S0-AXS-358

The Future of the Christian Church

by

Michael Ramsey

The Former Archbishop of Canterbury

and

Leon-Joseph Cardinal Suenens

Archbishop of Malines-Brussels

Morehouse-Barlow Co.

Wilton, Connecticut

© 1970 by Morehouse-Barlow Co.
78 Danbury Road, Wilton, Connecticut 06897
Printed in the United States of America
Library of Congress Catalog Card Number 79-138033
Standard Book Number 8192-1124-9

Third Printing, 1977

The authors gratefully thank the following publishers, who have kindly permitted them to use copyrighted material in their lectures:

Geoffrey Chapman Limited and Paulist/Newman Press for a passage from *Dialogue Between Christians* by Yves Congar; © Translation, 1966, Geoffrey Chapman Ltd.

Faber and Faber Ltd. and Harcourt Brace Jovanovich for permission to quote from T. S. Eliot's "Little Gidding," *Four Quartets,* © 1943 by T. S. Eliot.

FOREWORD

"I think it is daft — absolutely daft — that we should have to belong to separate ecclesiastical establishments." This was the spontaneous reaction of the Archbishop of Canterbury after two days of lecturing with Cardinal Suenens at the Seminar for Bishops at Trinity Institute in New York City on "The Future of the Christian Church." These lectures are presented here.

Just before he took his plane back to Belgium a few days after this seminar, the Cardinal called me to say how much he believed this event was of the Holy Spirit. He said characteristically, "We must be patient, but impatient."

The event which created these reactions was something of an incident in Church history. It was the first time that a primate of the Roman Catholic Church and the primate of another Christian communion had jointly given addresses since the Reformation. It might be suspected that Trinity Institute in issuing the invitation was contriving an ecumenical sensation. The fact is quite the opposite. These men are friends and the event developed naturally.

Trinity Institute is a theological institute for the Episcopal clergy nationally. Begun in 1967, sponsored by the Parish of Trinity Church in New York City, it functions as a place of meeting between the ministry of the Episcopal Church and men and women who are making an affirmative contribution in Christian thought. From the outset, it has offered an annual Seminar for Bishops in contemporary theology. The bishops have responded in strength. In fact, at this seminar, seventy-six were present, half of the active bishops of the Episcopal Church.

These lectures declare the theological dynamic for the future of the Church of Christ. They face that future in the hope which springs from the Christian faith. This is the reason why they will have a lasting importance. They do not contain fallible prognostications of what's coming next, or eventually, in a futile attempt to insulate churchmen against "future shock." They are based on the common affirmation of two realities of Christian experience which we share together in the communion of faith: the mystery of the Resurrection and the power of the Spirit. For this reason, they are full of expectation and hope. They do not regard the future of the Church just as something which is going to happen to Christians in a terrifying velocity of change. They regard the future of the Church as the will of the living Lord perpetually to be actualized by the power of the Spirit.

These lectures themselves, as the Cardinal pointed out, may be considered as one of the "surprises of the Holy Spirit": a decade ago they would have been impossible; five years ago, they would have been improbable. They represent more than another ecumenical event. They are beyond ecumenism; indeed, beyond dialogue. They disclose a unity of mind and spirit, a theological unity which already exists, waiting to be realised.

The two men were invited to give these lectures not because they are both such eminent ecclesiastical figures but because they are both men of faith. In fact, in the deepest sense, they reveal that they are theologians. As Metropolitan Anthony Bloom, the Russian Orthodox Archbishop in London, once remarked, "Theology is knowing God, not knowing about God, much less knowing what other people know about God." In this deepest sense, the Archbishop and the Cardinal are theologians.

Furthermore, they are performing the theological service of God as bishops. In these days, particularly in America, it is often forgotten that a bishop has a theological function to perform. He is consecrated to be both a teacher and a custodian of the faith. Too often, we think of a bishop simply as an administrator, as a personable political leader of the Church, or better, as a sacramental figure and pastor. There is yet a fuller Christian expectation. Some evidence of that expectation is strongly apparent in the fact that almost everything a bishop says is listened to because he is a bishop, no matter what prodigious nonsense he may utter. A bishop has a theological power even when he does not have a theological competence. The importance of these lectures is in part the fact that they are a prime example of the true function of the bishop theologically.

In reading these lectures, try to sense the situation in which they were delivered. In many senses it was a *meeting*.

This was a *meeting* of the Archbishop with the Cardinal. They had come together for this occasion, each to express his own deepest conviction about facing the future of the Church. There was no collusion, not even consultation, before the event. But they immediately discovered that they had arrived at essentially the same outline and approach independently. This was an immediate revelation of unity of understanding.

This was a *meeting* of two European primates with the bishops of the Episcopal Church in America. Our episcopate is very different in its nature from those of European churches. The pluralism of American Christianity, the relative newness of the nation, the predominantly technical development of the country, create a situation new in Christian history, new for a Christian episcopate.

This was a *meeting* of the Episcopal bishops with each other. Trinity Institute provides a place where Episcopal bishops can come together during a time of intense strain within the Church, without the pressure of critical debate and decision. They meet for these seminars to think about the essentials of the Christian faith. Their conversation with each other, the opportunity to know each other as friends, has proved an unplanned and unexpected value. On this occasion, it was infused with a sense of a greater belonging, or a greater fellowship in Christ, with the Christian episcopate across the barriers of disunion. The personalities of the Cardinal and the Archbishop made this vividly real.

Cardinal Suenens seems to have a strong affinity with Americans. In some ways, he appears like an American bishop, or even an efficient American businessman. His approach is basically pastoral, direct and practical. He is not ashamed of being moved and of moving his hearers with his simple evangelical faith. At the same time, he is unashamedly and discernably a convinced Roman Catholic. The popular image of him created by journalists as a man of controversy may mislead some to think of him as a radical reformer if not a reductionist. That is a slanderous misconception. He is first and foremost a man of powerful Christian conviction.

Dr. Ramsey vividly, even picturesquely, projects the image of the 100th Archbishop of Canterbury. He has a deceptively venerable appearance but a twinkling, mobile expression that reveals the alertness of his mind and spirit. At the seminar, he was doing what perhaps he enjoys most — being a theologian. He has already made what may prove to be the most substantial contribution in theology of any Anglican of his generation. He does not rest in this but is continually alive to what is happening now, as his comments here on current American theology reveal.

When I went to visit the Cardinal in Malines in

preparation for this event, as he took me into his study he said, "You will be glad to know that this is the room where the Malines Conversations occurred." Behind the occasion of these lectures stands the purpose of Cardinal Mercier, Cardinal Suenens' predecessor, Lord Halifax, the great Anglican layman, and the others who in the 1920's met for these Conversations. Their discussions, seeking a ground for understanding and unity between the Roman Catholic Church and Anglicanism, seemed to come to naught when they were suppressed from Rome. Their work is being fulfilled in this present. The fulfillment comes not in the wonderful expression of unity of spirit between the primates of the Church in Belgium and the Church of England; the fulfillment comes in a common facing of the future of the Christian Church in terms of a common Christian faith. Such is the power of the Spirit!

ROBERT E. TERWILLIGER
Director of Trinity Institute

New York City
July 31, 1970

CONTENTS

**The Archbishop
of
Malines-Brussels :**

Prologue

I. THE CHURCH IN HISTORY

At this moment the Church is living through difficult times. Things are in turmoil because everything is being questioned but the times are also vastly rich with hopes for the future. The crisis is evident, but opinions regarding the diagnosis of its cause are quite divergent. Whence comes this crisis? What is its true nature, and where is it leading us?

A correct analysis of the symptoms of a disease must precede any attempt at a cure; there is no other way. A man at sea can find out where he is if he uses a compass, observes which way the wind is blowing, and takes account of the currents and cross-currents which carry or impede his boat.

At the present time, the Church is like a ship exposed to every wind and battling through a sort of Bay of Biscay. One reason for this situation has nothing to do with the ship — it is caused by the condition of the sea. The Church exists in and for the world and as such lies open to the influence of the unprecedented changes which the world is experiencing. But there is also another reason, which belongs to the condition of the ship itself. Ever since the Council, the Church has been overhauling itself, not in some dry-dock but out in the open sea. The Church itself looks like some great shipping port at capacity production: passengers and crew experience daily to what degree they share the same lot and how intimately life on board ship concerns us all.

This heightened awareness of a common concern is a new thing. The sense of the co-responsibility of all Christians has been awakened. We have a long way to go before all its consequences are apparent, but a beginning has been made which cannot but grow greater. At this moment the words of Victor Hugo are particularly applicable, "Nothing is stronger than an idea whose hour has come." Whether we like it or not, the Church must adopt a new life style.

We are emerging from a long period, too long a period, during which for many Christians living in the Church meant little more than a passive inactivity and unthinking acceptance of Christianity which was more a sociological habit than personal conviction. Rather than accuse Vatican II, as some do, of having caused a torrential thaw, it would be better to find out why there was such a previous freeze-up which brought with it this inevitable consequence, and how to insure that icebergs will not form again in the future.

The difficulties which face us are many and

varied. Perhaps one of the most important of these is the fact that renewal is touching upon all aspects of the Church's life at once.

No aspect of renewal stands alone. For example, if we wish to see a greater exercise of collegiality on the part of the highest authority of the Church, then consistency demands that the image of the bishop within the local church or of the priest within each community be also re-thought in the same perspective. It is impossible to highlight the priesthood of the faithful without reconsidering the ministerial priesthood which, while always a part of the Church's life, must be lived in a different way. The creation of permanent deacons and certain new responsibilities given to lay people automatically imply a greater flexibility in our traditional structures and a pluralism of ecclesiastical functions. Thus, everything exercises a mutual influence on everything else and everyone must rethink his relationships to everyone else. But that cannot happen overnight.

Such a rethinking of mutual relations supposes that we are able to distinguish clearly what is essential and what is secondary and can be discarded, in what we have inherited from the past. We Christians, used to accepting indiscriminately as one whole the pure gold of the Gospel and the wrappings of human making, have not been trained to discern the difference. It is not easy to restore the interior of a gothic cathedral covered

with baroque or modern plaster and to recover its
original lines. To restore a cathedral like some
Viollet le Duc requires more than momentary
enthusiasm.

I will be speaking later about a rich insight
which is expressed in the conciliar document on
Ecumenism when it uses the phrase "hierarchy of
truths." This expression is extremely valuable in
any ecumenical dialogue while remaining a permanent challenge to every Christian to reflect
upon what is the very core of Christianity and
what is peripheral. This is especially applicable to
all that has been added to Revelation by theologians, moralists, and preachers throughout the
ages, who have at times moved too hastily beyond
the veil of mystery.

A tree grows if it is pruned once in a while.
When the excess growth is cut, the sap rises more
abundantly in the main branches. But it takes a
sure hand to prune without killing, and it takes a
healthy optimism to have confidence in the power
of Spring when one sees the pruned branches all
around.

Today's renewal, so delicate to bring about, so
burgeoning with life, is facing a great challenge: it
is the very depth of the conversion demanded of
us to be faithful to the Gospel with all this entails.
We are called to be faithful to what the world
expects of us and this cannot be realized without
pain, disappointments, and contradictions. Life is
made up of tensions seeking a balance. The
difficulties of the journey are the price we must

pay to discover new horizons. The very depth of the work undertaken by the Holy Spirit within us, individually and collectively, requires time and patience.

As we wait for the continuity of the generations to be established, and for the Holy Spirit to triumph over the sin which is an obstacle to Him in each one of us, it seems to me that it would be a service to the Christian of today, who is en route toward the twenty-first century, to show that the Church is a reality situated within history. The time in which we live becomes more understandable to us if we join it to yesterday and try to link it with tomorrow, just as in discovering the position of a ship we must calculate its latitude and longitude on the map. If we understand the relationship of the Church to time in general, it will help us understand the Church in relation to our time. We cannot but profit from viewing the Church thus plunged within the very heart of history, and not like some abstract, unchangeable reality untouched by time. We have already suffered too much from a static view of the Church defined juridically as a 'perfect society.'

Thanks be to God, we do not tend to look upon the Church any more in juridical categories, but rather as a living thing animated by the presence and life of Christ which is making its way from Easter to the coming of the Lord. The Church is a pilgrim walking through time and history, going from stage to stage along a way as yet incomplete. The history of the Exodus teaches us that God does not like to give to His people great supplies of provisions for the journey but rather to be with them and provide them with manna for the day. We had become accustomed to accumulating any number of constraining accessories and to building houses of stone and cement, rather than being happy with tents that can be folded and moved and allow us always to be ready to go on.

A Church which has placed itself once again within history is more likely to awaken in its members a deeper sense of freedom and flexibility and an understanding of our obligation to remain faithful to the past, to the present, and to the future. This three-fold fidelity is at once the glory and the most radiant crown of the Church.

II. *THE CHURCH AND THE PAST*

The Church in all its being is rooted in the past. It must remain faithful to its beginning, to its principle of continuity, and to its tradition, if it does not want to deny its own reality. The Church is nourished by that profound continuity which links it to its origin, as a tree lives by its roots. But it is important that the tree itself be not confused with those outgrowths which have sprung up at the foot of the tree during the course of time. Obviously it is not easy to distinguish that which pertains to authentic theology and dogma and that which results from sociological or cultural factors. A real theologian knows this better than anyone else and tries always to be aware of his own subjective attitude.

It is precisely an amazing ignorance of history,

which one finds among conservatives, that makes conservatism so sure of itself and so closed to dialogue. Conservatives venture to 'dogmatize' well beyond the limits of dogma and to canonize opinions that are the products of a particular period of history. All this is rendered easier for them by the fact that such people lack any historical perspective.

History is not only 'the mistress of life'; it is also the guide to research. By the very fact that it can place a reality in context, making it relative to other factors and rendering conclusions more modest, circumspect, and balanced, it acts as a guideline along the road, indicating where to slow down and be careful. History teaches the art of perspective and proportion. How many arguments could be rescued from an impasse if one side or the other would agree to go back, to search out the beginnings, to investigate together complimentary truths and hidden preconceptions! If I wish to really understand the meaning and importance of a past council, then I must understand the context in which that council occurred, the problems which it had to face, its 'Sitz im Leben,' its fears, its preoccupations, and its areas of ignorance.

History is absolutely indispensable for the Church in order to keep it truly faithful to its origins. But history also confers other riches on us by giving us in addition a good lesson in humility and confidence. We get a lesson in humility because history shows us vividly how we carry our treasures in earthen vessels. But we also learn confidence because we see how profoundly God is at work in the Church through all its human inadequacy. We touch upon the principle already proposed by Gamaliel when, according to the Acts of the Apostles, he said to the tribunal which wished to condemn Peter and John, "If this enterprise, this movement of theirs, is of human origin, it will break up of its own accord: but if it does in fact come from God you will not only be unable to destroy them, but you might find yourselves fighting against God" (Acts 5:39). This apologetic argument is always valid.

Continuity with the past is a primary duty for the Church. We could say that it is from there that it derives the sap of its life.

The remote origin of the Church is found in the history of Israel. With the people of the ancient covenant, the Church goes back through the course of centuries. The Church never accepted a radical break with its Jewish past and it condemned Marcionism as a heresy when that movement proposed such a rupture. At Vatican II when the Fathers of the Council felt themselves obliged to make a declaration which was favorable to the Jews, their purpose was not only to render justice, but also to express the fidelity of the Church to itself.

If the remote origin of the Church is found within the ancient people of God, its direct source is found in those events that occurred twenty centuries ago: facts which are, at one and the same time, and in an indissoluble manner, both history and mystery. The Church does not confuse history with historicism. She knows well enough that the whole reality from which she lives cannot be reduced to the dimensions and methods proper to the science of history. The very richness of the objective, original reality, transcends our neat compartments: the same reality is viewed under both the light of history and the light of faith.

However, the Church opposes and will always oppose the attitude that sees the approach of faith and the approach of history as incompatible. It cannot admit that lack of continuity which modern liberal exegetes, before, with, and after Rudolph Bultmann, have attempted to establish between the Jesus of history and the Christ of faith. The decisive factor which gave rise to Christianity is the historical Jesus of the Gospels and not the paschal faith of his disciples, even if these Gospels themselves come to us from the post-Resurrection community. If we make of the paschal event a purely interior happening, which occurred within the souls of the disciples, touched off by a process that itself remains inexplicable, we fail to understand the very foundations of faith. It is good to see the reaction against such an 'interiorization' of the paschal reality growing ever stronger, even among Rudolph Bultmann's disciples, such as Wolfhart Pannenberg, and the proponents of the Theology of Hope, about which we will speak later.

Christianity can never be reduced to a subjective projection, collective or individual, to an ideology or a dialectic. It is first and foremost an

event, a person: Jesus Christ acknowledged as
Lord. A Christian is not a philosopher who has
opted for a certain explanation of the universe,
but a man who has met in his own life Jesus of
Nazareth, crucified on Good Friday and risen from
the tomb. The cry of Claudel, "Behold, all of a
sudden you are Somebody," is the cry of faith for
all generations, past and future. However, if the
Christian is a man who derives his life from the
past, who lives because of a unique event in the
past, it is not as though he comes in contact with
that past across a void of twenty centuries. The
past comes to him because it is always living in the
Church. In saying to His disciples, "Behold, I am
with you always, even to the end of the world,"
the Lord intended to assure them of His presence
in the Church and to abolish, between himself and
us, all that the past normally implies in distance
and estrangement. In Christ, the past is overcome.
Through Him and in Him, the Church comes to us
as the heir of a past which is living and radiant in
its present reality.

The Christian of today moves toward his Lord,
not only with his own personal faith, isolated and
sometimes vacillating, but with the faith of the
whole Church, the faith of yesterday and that of
today. He believes as the heir of the believers of
yesterday. Just before receiving the Body of the
Lord, the Church puts upon our lips this great
prayer, "Lord, look not upon our sins, but upon
the faith of your Church." It is with this ecclesial
faith that I come to meet the Son of God. I believe
with the faith of the patriarchs and prophets; with

the faith of Mary and the apostles and martyrs, the doctors, the confessors, the mystics, and the saints. It is the power of each poor Christian that he knows himself to be part of a great continuous whole, a link in a great chain welded to the Lord through those who have gone before us. It is always a great moment for me when, during an ordination liturgy, we sing the Litany of the Saints. It is good to feel oneself united with our forefathers in the faith, of whom we ask a mediating presence for the sake of the man to be ordained. This communion, which reaches out through the centuries and is joined to the glorious Church, is a deep breath of fresh air for us. It is like some pause on the plateau of a mountain: there, before such an horizon, we breath better.

In this chain that joins us to the past, there is a special link that commands our faith. We say in the Credo, "I believe in the Apostolic Church," that is to say our faith derives from the privileged witness of the Apostles. Built upon the Rock of Peter and the foundation of the Twelve, faith finds its anchor there and begins from this point, which is its source of transmission, reference, and fidelity.

The tradition that stands above all others as the peak of a mountain dominates the landscape and acts as a watershed is the tradition that rests upon the Word of God as lived and transmitted through the ministry of the Apostolic college. That which St. Paul wrote to Timothy, who was beginning his apostolic responsibility, remains valid for all times:

"Keep as your pattern the sound teaching you have heard from me, in the faith and love that are in Christ Jesus. You have been trusted to look after something precious; guard it with the help of the Holy Spirit who lives in us" (II Tim. 1:13-14). These words apply to every Christian who is essentially one of the 'faithful.'

At a time when the ship is being battered we ought to offer to God and to His Church a fidelity that is ever more pure and stable. Our fidelity ought to be purer because it relies no longer on the sociological underpinnings of a Christian culture that is disappearing, but upon God Himself, who is experienced in our more personal concerned and apostolic commitment. Our fidelity is more stable because we must go through and beyond the weaknesses of the Church and know how to recognize and love its true face.

Despite the deep wrinkles on the face of his mother, an adult knows how to see in her look the eternal youth of a love that never grows old. When we were children we thought that our mother had the answer for everything. When we grew up we discovered her limitations; but this never diminished our love, it only made it more deeply real. As Christians who have grown up, we know that we owe to the Church the very best that is in us. And that is sufficient reason why she remains for all of us, despite her 'wrinkles,' our Mother, the Holy Church.

III. *THE CHURCH AND THE PRESENT*

We would have a truncated image of the

Church if we considered it only as turned toward the past. The Church is preeminently a reality of the present. If the salvation of the world is a fact accomplished once and for all by the Passion and Resurrection, redemption goes on each day as it applies the fruits of this mystery to each person. The past and the present are mutually interpenetrating: the past is actualized by the present, which in turn flows out from the past. Pascal once said, "Christ is in agony throughout the centuries and we must not sleep during this time." The mystery of salvation is as great as the centuries, and it is lived out before our very eyes. When a priest holds up the consecrated Host before the faithful and says, "This is the Lamb of God Who takes away the sins of the world," he recalls to all that the paschal mystery is always being worked out.

The same can be said for the actuality of the Gospel message. The Church lives from the past but it is completely oriented toward the present, toward the opportune moment that the New Testament calls the *kairos*. It offers God's message as Good News that keeps its freshness and youth for each generation. Lacordaire once defined a Christian in this magnificent phrase, "A Christian is a man to whom Jesus Christ has confided other men." These men who have been confided to us are not the men of yesterday; they are the people of right now, our next door neighbors, our fellow workers, our fellow students, all those whom we meet.

Devotion and respect in regard to the past have nothing in common with rigid lack of change or the respect properly accorded a museum piece. The Church must always draw from her treasure, "the new and the old." She must be actual, incarnate, and present in the tangible reality of human life in all its dimensions. The Council vividly recalled for us our duty to read and understand the signs of the times, *Vox temporum vox Dei.* That motto is still true. Today, God still speaks in and through events; we must believe in and bring about the constant interplay between the living God and men of flesh and blood. Someone once asked Karl Barth, "What do you do to prepare your Sunday sermon?" Barth answered, "I take the Bible in one hand and the daily newspaper in the other." To see events in their relationship to God is part of the mediating mission of the Church. It is a daily and difficult task, for new problems are continually arising.

The Gospel is not an answer book. It offers 'Words of Life' that speak to the primal experiences of man. It is an unfailing spring of living water and that is why, in the Church, the reading of its sacred pages is a constant duty.

The Church cannot afford to canonize the past. We must be on our guard against a certain kind of "primitivism" about which I will be speaking later. This primitivism will consist in wishing to recreate some past age of the church as being the norm of its whole life. There is no golden age that ought to be restored. In this sense, we should have no nostalgia, even for the primitive Church. We must not fool ourselves: the picture of the primitive Christian communities is far from idyllic and it contains diverging tendencies as different as Jewish and Hellenic cultures. A reading of the Acts of the Apostles shows us how free the Apostles were in adopting ways and means to suit their mission. Fidelity to tradition does not mean materially copying their efforts, but trying to do what they tried to do.

Authentic development of the Church implies growth in maturity. As I grow up, my past always remains mine, but with the passage of time I see it in a different light. I am at this moment much more than a total of previous strata. Authentic tradition, which is distinguished from pseudo-traditions, is not a dominance or imperial rule that the past exercises over the present, but a living assimilation of the past by the present. In the 'today' of the Church, the past is at once contained and transcended.

Every once in a while, I ask myself what I would have been and what I would have believed as a Christian if, instead of living in 1970, I lived in 1870 or 1770 or 1670, and so on. Every time I end my little meditation with an enthusiastic thanks to the Lord for the present time in which he has willed to place me.

If we should never yield to the temptation of primitivism we should be equally on our guard against the mirage of "presentism," which is a sort of indiscriminate canonization of the present. This is the temptation that lies in wait for those who, in their enthusiasm to stress the church's obligation to be present to the world, either forget or minimize that which is always and irreducibly part of Christianity of any time.

The Constitution on the Church in the Modern World requires that we read the signs of the times but it never intends to make the terms *Church* and *World* completely synonymous or to oblige us to change with every passing fashion of the day. Nor did the Council intend simply the translation of an eternal message into modern terms. Rather it offered an appeal to re-read the Gospel in faith with the light of the Holy Spirit while living the experience of a man of today. What is asked of us is a re-reading with a view to a new hearing of that Word of God which is always living and actual. We must be free enough to understand today what the Spirit is saying to the Churches. The Church is not faithful to itself unless it is ready at every moment for the surprises of the Holy Spirit and the unexpectedness of God.

What men are waiting for from the Church, whether they realize it or not, is that the Church of today show them the Gospel. Our contemporaries want to meet the Christ who is alive today; they want to see him with their eyes and touch him with their hands. Like those pilgrims who approached Philip one day, they say to us, "We wish to see Jesus." Our contemporaries want a meeting face to face with Christ. The challenge for us as Christians is that they demand to see Christ in each one of us; they want us to reflect Christ as clearly as a pane of glass transmits the rays of the sun. Whatever is opaque and besmirched in us disfigures the face of Christ in the Church. What the unbeliever reproaches us with is not that we are Christians, but that we are not Christian enough: that is the tragedy. When Gandhi read the Gospels, he was deeply moved and wanted to become a Christian, but the sight of the Christians around him stopped him and made him withdraw. Such is the great weight of our responsibility.

IV. *THE CHURCH AND THE FUTURE*

Our vision of the Church would not be complete unless we consider the Church, again in that totality of its being, as turned and tending toward the future.

Modern man is to a surprising degree preoccupied with the future. So profoundly influenced is he by this sense of the future, that he has made a science of prediction. Tomorrow and the day after tomorrow fascinate him.

At one time man sought to unlock the secret of the future by consulting the stars. Today, rather than force the door of the impenetrable, or seek to divine the future, man tries to create it, to invent it, to discover techniques to control his movement through time. Within the heart of the man of today, anguished and troubled as it may sometimes be, there is a great hope, which he is seeking to unleash.

Modern man is living by a temporal messianic hope; the Church lives by a theological or God-centered hope. The Church offers to men a hope that goes beyond anything the eyes of man have seen or human ears have heard; it is nothing else than that which God himself has prepared for those whom he loves.

Contemporary man and the Church have found a meeting place: it is their common attention to the future. In his book, *The Principle of Hope,* the famous Marxist philosopher Ernst Bloch has written these words: "Where there is hope, there is religion." His formula may be ambiguous, but it has a valid meaning. It should not be surprising therefore that this same Ernst Bloch has enriched the thought of those theologians who have so strongly reaffirmed the eschatological aspect of the Church: that aspect of "*en route* to the future."

It is of the utmost importance that the false opposition between the Church and the future be broken down. We can never accept the oft-repeated phrase, "the Church lives by its memories; the world by its hope." It is absolutely essential that the Gospel be presented to the world as a hope. This preoccupation of modern man is not completely new; Kant has already posed his three famous questions: "What can I know?" "What must I do?" "What can I hope?" His *Critique of Pure Reason*, his *Critique of Practical Reason*, and his *Critique of Aesthetic Judgment* are his attempts to answer this three-fold question. The third question, "What can I hope?" is found at the heart of modern philosophy with a new urgency, but it has also forced us to focus attention upon a dimension of Christianity that is all too frequently forgotten. Christianity is a religion turned toward the future, moving toward the *parousia*, toward the final meeting with the Lord.

In accepting openness to the future, the Church will regain the attention of youth who are preoccupied with the world to be created and who are at once fascinated and awed by tomorrow. From now on this world is, to a large degree, in our hands. Nature will never again appear to man as an abstract fatality, as the rigid raw material for his creativity, but rather as a supple medium, which he can use at his discretion and include in his plans. Modern man is fascinated by the world he must create, not by a ready-made world that he was forced to respect and oftentimes feared, a world that, even yesterday, seemed to dictate its laws to him while remaining hostile to him. We are far from that time when Philip II of Spain, wishing to make the Tagus river navigable, submitted his project to a commission. The commission rejected the proposal, giving as its reason, "If God had wished that this river be navigable, he would have accomplished it with a single word." As a conclusion the commission said that, for the future, "it would be a rash trespass upon the rights of God if human hands were to dare improve a work left unfinished by God for reasons beyond our ken." Our world is at the other extreme from such an idea. We Christians must, as it were, form a meeting place between the transcendence of God and the future of the world, without con-

fusing God with some immanent earthly future as
if God were the term of some incredibly complex
cosmic evolution.

Whatever shows the Church as a community
moving toward its final destiny, toward God who
will be 'all in all,' toward the glorified Christ, has a
particular power of speaking to our time. We
ourselves must rediscover the God of the Bible;
the God of Abraham, Isaac, and Jacob; and not the
God of the philosophers. We must free ourselves
from those aspects of Greek philosophy that viewed the universe as a world enclosed upon itself,
forever destined to be a cyclic whirlpool with no
life movement toward the future. We must rediscover the personal God of the Bible. He is not the
God who wishes to reveal to us first and foremost
a series of theological propositions and theses, but
the God of that promise which commits us to the
future, the God who reveals Himself to us as a
Love that is personal, spontaneous, unmerited,
and irrevocable.

It is in this perspective that we can locate the
Church between the 'already' of Easter and the
'not yet' of the *parousia*. In the Church, the past is
always actual and the future is already present. In
the Church, tradition means perpetual renewal
and evolution means continuity. In the Church,
there lives Christ who is "the same yesterday,
today, and forever."

The Gospel will be an immense life-force for the
world that will come if we only know how to show
it forth in the right way. "A message becomes

believable to the degree that it shows itself able to open up to hope and to the future." These words of Kaspers are significant. The Gospel is credible, and the Church will be accepted and listened to, to the degree that the Church is faithful to the Gospel and knows how to speak to men in the language of hope and translate that language visibly by her joy. For the sign of a Christian is joy. It is the sure test of the hope he claims is his: that hope of which St. Peter said, "Simply reverence the Lord Christ in your hearts and always have your answer ready for people who ask you the reason for the hope that you have" (I Pet. 3:15).

The world is longing for a breath of fresh air, for an alleluia that can free us. Harvey Cox in his recent book, *The Feast of Fools,* has become the spokesman for a powerful current of thought and desire that is stirring at this moment. His book itself is a sign of the times: it reserves a large place for joy, humor, and fantasy in a world too serious about its own techniques. The Christian more than anyone can answer this appeal; it belongs to him to reveal to men that joy is a flower that can only open up and last when planted in the soil of a hope that is born of God and rests in God.

**The Archbishop
of
Canterbury :**

1. Death and Resurrection

In our thoughts about the future of the Christian Church, we need to set the matter in the context of our faith in God. We say in the Creed, "I believe in one Holy, Catholic, and Apostolic Church," and in so doing we affirm that the Church is a part of "the faith" in which we believe. It is made by God, given by God. We value the sacraments and the ministerial order of the Church as signs of the givenness of the Church in history, of the meaning of the Church as a sacrament of the eternal in the midst of time.

Yet we know that this divine gift is mediated through frail, sinful, and fallible men and women. The Church is human as well as divine. It is divine because the principle of its life is the risen Lord present in His body through the Holy Spirit. It is human inasmuch as its members are capable of sins and failings which grievously thwart and hinder the divine life within it. Hence in history the divine judgment again and again falls upon the

Church in its human part, and exhibits its members as what the prophets of old called "a hissing and a reproach." Yet again and again after a time of judgment, God has raised up a remnant of faithful people and used them for the execution of His purpose. It is in virtue, not of any quality inherent in the Church's members, but of God's faithfulness in judging and raising up, that the Church continues and "the gates of death shall not prevail against it." We who are bishops will remind ourselves that we belong both to the sin of the Church and to the divine ordering of the Church. While our sins wound the head of the Church and hurt the people who are its members, our office, as a commission from Christ, is a sign of the Church's divine mission, rebuking our sins and reminding us that we are here only as Christ's slaves and the people's servants.

When therefore we say that we believe in the Church, we do so only and always in terms of our belief in the God who judges and raises up. The mistake of ecclesiasticism through the ages has been to believe in the Church as a kind of thing-in-itself. The apostles never regarded the Church as a thing-in-itself. Their faith was in God, who had raised Jesus from the dead, and they knew the power of His Resurrection to be at work in them and in their fellow believers despite the unworthiness of them all. That is always the true nature of belief in the Church. It is a laying-hold on the power of the Resurrection. And because it is that, it is always on the converse side *death*: death to self; death to wordly hopes; death to self-

sufficiency; death to any kind of security for the
Church or for Christianity, other than the security
of God and the Resurrection. "We have this
treasure in earthen vessels, to show that the
transcendent power belongs to God and not to
us" (II Cor. 4:7).

We say this. We think we know this. But again
and again we lapse into trying to make the Church
credible on grounds other than those of the God
of the Cross and the Resurrection. We try to find
the Church's security, and our own security in the
Church, in false ways. I think of three familiar ways
of false security: there are the false security of
religion, the false security of theology, the false
security of activisim.

There is the false security of religion. We have
had in the West much 'religious prosperity': large
congregations, devotional fervor, lovely music,
the enjoyment of a genuine religious culture. This
may be a true and authentic outcome of the
Gospel. Yet it may become a self-contained realm
and with it there may be the tacit acceptance of
assumptions about human society which are not
those of the New Testament. So secure may
religion feel itself that it may run on for long
periods without criticizing itself, without sub-
mitting itself to the judgment of the Gospel. And
the genuine Christian virtues it produces may
make it the more blind in its security. Then the
draft comes. It came in England several decades
ago. It is perhaps beginning to come in America
today. When it comes, our religious security begins to fail us. We discover what F. D. Maurice

meant when he said, "We have been dosing our people with religion, when what they want is not that but the living God."

If we are aware that this is our situation, what do we do? Too often we clutch at our religious security and try to refurbish it and protect it. But what ought we to do? We ought to suspect that God's judgment is falling on us, to try to discover why, and to look for our security to the God who, ever faithful to His Church, exposes painfully, judges, and raises up.

Then, there is the false security of theology in the Church. Now theology is a precious gift and God gave it. Theology is indispensable for the Church and for every member of the Church. But the object of faith is not theology but the God whose theology it is. We can be sound in the theology of the Bible, grasping correctly the Biblical words and the Biblical thought-forms, Biblical Theology with a capital *B* and a capital *T*. Yet our Biblical Theology can be held in a kind of vacuum, without sensitivity to the human context in which theology comes alive. So too, it can be used as a thing for the mind, without the knowledge that comes through prayer and contemplation. In those ways theology, divorced both from the social context and from the inner life, can become a thing-in-itself, and be substituted for the God who gave it. The substitution can be made equally by Barthians and by Liberals, by Catholics and by Protestants, each after his own kind.

When that happens, there comes a time of sickness and deadness in theology and men can begin to talk about God being dead. What then? The way of faith is not to try to bolster up old theology in the old ways, nor is it to abandon theology in the quest of a kind of Godless Christianity. The way of faith is rather to go into the darkness without fearing, and in the darkness to meet again the God who judges and raises the dead.

Then, there is the false security of practical good works in the Church. Now good works are the urgent outcome of faith and the lack of them may be often an occasion for divine judgment on the Church. There can be no true faith which does not overflow in actions of compassion and human reconciliation. The Church must be the servant of humanity. But woe to the Church if it thinks it can justify itself to the world, and find its own security, in a successful program of philanthropy. It was such a justification of His own mission which our Lord decisively rejected as He moved towards the Cross for which He had been sent for the world's redemption. The Church is called to serve without ceasing, but never to commend itself to the world by providing what the world would most like and approve on the world's own terms. When the Church tries to commend itself in this way it can do good, it can win admiration for a while, but it can lose the power to lead men to repentance, to divine forgiveness, and to the God of the Resurrection.

These forms of false security are familiar: security by religion, security by theology, security by activism. The pendulum sometimes swings be-

tween them. Not for a moment dare we belittle
religion, for it is the creature's communion with
his creator; or theology, for it is the truth of God's
word; or good works, for without them faith is
dead. But each is God's gift, and not itself the end
of faith. Our faith is in GOD, a faith that is always
on one side frailty, self-distrust, penitence, death;
and on the other side power, glory, resurrection.
When times of leanness come we shall put ourselves under God's judgment and ask that our
religion, our theology, our good works, and we
ourselves may be humbled and cleansed. Then
into the darkness the light of Resurrection breaks.
We cease to be confident and complacent about
our religion, but we begin to pray with the awe
and humility of children. We are less proud of our
theology, but we allow the Word of God to find us
in new and unexpected ways. We cease to commend our activism, but we spend ourselves in
serving with the mind of unprofitable servants.
The difference is that God is alive for us, and we
now help other people to find God alive for them.

I find the meaning of the Church in relation to
the God of the Resurrection drawn out, as nowhere so powerfully, in the Epistles of St. Paul to
the Corinthians, and specially in the first six chapters of the Second Epistle. The story of St. Paul and
Corinth is a kind of epitome of nineteen centuries
and more of Christian history in miniature. It gives
a picture in which we all have a place. The
Christians in Corinth were "called to be saints
together with all those who in every place call on
the name of our Lord Jesus Christ" (I Cor. 1:2).

They are saints indeed, and lovely fruits of the Holy Spirit are seen in them. Then, we read on. Divisions, quarrels, intellectual perversions, moral scandals; the apostle is ashamed of his converts, they bring shame on the name of Christ. But God does not fail them. There is death, and there is resurrection.

Whereas I Corinthians gives the external picture of the Church in its glory and its shame, II Corinthians discloses in agony and ecstasy the inner meaning. And the inner meaning is that, because the power whereby the Church is sustained is the Resurrection, the members of the Church recapture this power only by being brought near to the Cross. When their tasks are beyond them, when they know their frailty and are ready to share Christ's suffering, then life is present and life presses on in the winning of souls and the building of the Church in unity. I recall some passages:

> Such is the confidence that we have towards God through Christ. Not that we are sufficient of ourselves to claim anything as coming from us.

> What we preach is not ourselves but Jesus Christ as Lord, and ourselves as your servants for Jesus' sake.

> We have this treasure in earthen vessels, to show that the transcendent power belongs to God and not to us. We are afflicted in every way, but not crushed, perplexed but not driven to despair, persecuted but not forsaken, struck down but not destroyed, always bearing in the body the dying of Jesus that the life also of Jesus may be manifested in our body.

So death is at work in us, but life in you.

This slight momentary affliction is preparing for us
an eternal weight of glory beyond all comparison.

As imposters and yet true, as unknown and yet well
known, as dying and behold we live, as poor yet
making many rich, as having nothing and yet
possessing all things.

What is it that these words describe? They are a
key to St. Paul's understanding of his apostleship
and of the Church. It might be thought that they
describe the experience of persecution but that
does not really fit the historical situation. It might
be thought that they describe a particular ascetic
vocation but that is not in view. No, these tremen-
dous words about death and life have a more
catholic and lasting application. They describe the
essential relation of a pastor to his people, and of
the people to their pastor, and of the Church to
the world and the Church to its Lord. Above all
they describe the meaning of faith — for faith
means to look for no security in oneself, no
security in one's fellow Christians, no security in
any of the world's props or in any of the Church's
props, but security only in a nearness to the Cross
and to the Resurrection beyond it. Such is the God
in whom Christians believe. Such is the Church
with the light of Calvary and Easter upon it.

It is in the midst of such a faith that we cherish
our hopes about the Church's future. What hopes
does the New Testament encourage us to have?

The hope that rings through the apostolic writings is primarily the hope of the vision of God in

heaven, the hope of the coming of Christ in glory, the hope also of the coming of the reign of God. "Come, Lord Jesus." The Church worships, serves, preaches the Gospel, draws men and women into fellowship with God, with its hope set not upon its own destiny but upon its Lord as it awaits His coming. Yet in one of the apostolic writings, the Epistle to the Ephesians, the hope is in a measure focused upon the Church itself, as Christ's body and Christ's fullness; and the hope is that its members will grow into the completeness of His manhood, that mankind will be united in His body, and that the Church, as Christ's bride, will be found without spot or wrinkle. Such then will be our hopes for the Church, subordinate always to the hope for heaven and the hope for the coming of Christ.

We need however to remind ourselves that the New Testament while it bids us hope firmly and hope joyfully, nowhere encourages us to expect that the coming of the Kingdom of God will happen in a steady progression. It was indeed characteristic of much theology in the last century and the early years of the present century to think of the Kingdom of God in that way. Mankind would become gradually more religious, more ethical in its behavior, more educated, more just in its social and economic life and so, through the steady growth of religion and knowledge, the Kingdom of God would come. But neither our Lord nor the apostles encourage such an idea. Rather do parts of their teaching suggest that there may be a series of catastrophic happenings in which evil shows itself with new power and, perhaps, there will be a final manifestation of evil in horrible forms, before Christ finally triumphs. To say this, is not to lessen the confidence of the Christian hope, it is only to insist that it is always hope in the God of Calvary and Easter.

Nor does the New Testament encourage us to suppose that if only the Church were really Christlike and really efficient in doing its work then people everywhere would be readily converted. The 'if only' idea can be very misleading. We dare not overlook the words of St. Paul: "If our gospel is veiled it is veiled to those who are perishing. In their case the God of this world has blinded the minds of the unbelieving to keep them from seeing the light of the gospel of the glory of God in the face of Jesus Christ" (II Cor. 4:3-4). The simplicity of the gospel does not mean that it can be easily grasped by those who are worldly and impenitent. It means that it poses the issue in a sharp and simple way and, in so doing, it divides mankind. At present, because the Church is not Christlike enough, the division is often at the wrong line: there are some inside the Church who would be outside the Church if the Church were more Christlike, and there are some outside the Church who would be drawn inside if it were a more Christlike Church. If the Church bore its witness more faithfully, certain issues would be seen more sharply and simply.

The Church will not be afraid to be a force which divides as well as unites, if its faith in God is sure. Faith will open our eyes to the presence of

God in unsuspected ways. In the secular world and in the technological sciences God may be there, there to show us new apprehensions of Himself and to give us new tasks to do. In the darkness of contemporary perplexities of thought God may be there, there to show us through darkness a new grasp of Himself. In the sufferings of our fellows God may be there, there for us to serve Him in Christ's brothers. In the catastrophes of the world God may be there, there in judgment to show mankind the outcome of its own evil choices. And in the joy and serenity of those who serve Him in faith, God may be there, the giver of a joy from heaven and a peace which surpasses every human contrivance.

In all these ways the perplexities that confront us are so many opportunities for faith to show itself. But to learn of God in new ways is not to abandon those that are old, if their claim rests not upon their being old but upon their being time- less. The worship and contemplation of God be- long not to man's immaturity but to man's timeless privilege as God's child and creature with heaven as his goal. And the sacrament of the body and blood of Christ in the Eucharist belongs to the timeless participation of Christians in His death and resurrection. There the Church renews its faith in the God who is true and living.

2. The Church and the World

In the last few years the phrase 'the Servant Church' has been very prominent. It makes a strong appeal as it suggests a Church that sets aside worldly pomp, cares not for itself but for others, and tries to follow the humility of Christ. In the year 1968 the phrase was much used both at the Assembly of the World Council of Churches at Uppsala and at the Lambeth Conference of Anglican Bishops. But like other phrases which have become popular it can bring confusion as well as truth. You remember how meticulous Bishop Westcott of Durham used to be about the use of New Testament words, and the story is told that when he was asked, "Are you saved?" he replied, "Do you mean *sotheis* or *sozomenos* or *sesosmenos?*" I think that if Bishop Westcott had been with us at the last Lambeth Conference and had heard the speeches about the Servant Church he might have intervened to ask "do you mean *diakonos* or *doulos?*" The distinction between those two concepts is important.

There is first the word *diakonos,* with the verb *diakonein,* reproduced in our word *deacon.* It is a functional word, meaning one who renders acts of service to other people and in particular the service of waiting at table. At the last supper Jesus uses the imagery to show the apostles the supremacy of the service of others. "For which is the greater, one who sits at table, or one who serves? Is it not the one who sits at table? But I am among you as one who serves" (Luke 22:27). Thus authority is rooted in humility, and the practical service by Christians of one another and of all is a paramount duty. It is this which is in mind, and rightly so, when people speak of the Servant Church. The Church will follow Christ in the outgoing service of human needs, the poor, the hungry, the sick, the disinherited, with no motive but the compassion drawn from Christ Himself and with the humility which banishes patronage or possessiveness.

Yet it is all too easy for the false conception to seep in, that the Church exists to serve the world by giving the world what the world likes and wants and thinks it needs most on its own assumptions. The Bishop of Durham, Dr. Ian Ramsey, has aptly said in his essay in the book *All One Body,* "While I am all for developing the image of the Servant Church, I think it is sometimes used in such a context as to suggest the Church constantly groveling before society, constantly looking over its shoulder, and guiding its life by what it thinks people would like to see it do." The Church needs to be challenging the world's assumptions and showing that the world's greatest need is to be brought in humility and repentance into the love and obedience of God. Nor can we forget that our Lord's supreme service of the world was not His healing of the sick and His feeding of the hungry but His death on the Cross, for He "came not to be served but to serve, and to give his life a ransom for many" (Mark 10:45).

Here the word *doulos* comes into view. It is a word which does not describe the performing of functions so much as a relationship to another. It is the relationship of the slave: to be possessed by another utterly, with no claims, no rights, no earnings, no independent status of one's own. And the Other who thus possesses a man is God. The apostle is Christ's slave; and Christ Himself took the form of a slave and became obedient even unto death *(cf.* Phil. 2:1-8). This aspect of the Servant Church must not be forgotten. While it serves human needs the Church lives a Godward life, possessed by God and witnessing that only when lives are utterly possessed by God do they find their true freedom. That is the Church's message to the world. Of course the image of the slave can mislead, and no image in itself suffices. The image of the slave blends with the images of son, friend, priest, and many others in describing the God-man relationship. So let our serving of the world as *diakonoi* be always interwoven with our bondage to Christ as His *douloi,* as we witness to the sovereignty of God, whom to obey is true freedom.

What then is the true relation between the Church and the world, bearing in mind both these aspects of the servant concept? I would describe two contrasted views of the relation which I believe to be misleading; then I would ask if there is a more excellent way, which can give validity and significance to our ministry.

First, there has been the view that the Church has the role of being the society which represents the claims of religion within the community. This view could be expressed thus. "The community is occupied with many things: family life, civic life, work, leisure, amusement, art, science, industry, commerce, politics. But there is something more important than all these, namely religion. God's first great commandment demands that God be loved supremely and put first. Therefore the Church puts God first, by insisting on the primacy of worship and by drawing people into fellowship with God within the worshipping community, as well as by proclaiming the gospel of salvation through faith in God. Of course, if people really put God first it will have an effect on the community and its problems, since the solution of all problems is to have converted Christian lives. But we need not, in preaching the Gospel and in building up the life of the Church, press these social corollaries too far, since the great evil in the modern world is the neglect of God and religion and the Church must never relax its preoccupation with what matters most."

Is that an unfair description of a religious attitude which has been very familiar? Perhaps it is an attitude more half-consciously assumed than consciously stated or worked out. I suspect that it was in large part my own attitude when I began my ministry as a priest forty years ago. It is an attitude which does not exclude a genuine social concern, for inevitably the practice of the first great commandment overflows into the practice of the second. Yet there was, and is, something unsatisfactory about this viewpoint. It may fail to touch the life of real persons, because, both in the preaching of the Gospel and in the building up of Christian life, it deals not with persons as they really are but with persons somewhat abstracted from their real existence into a realm of religion. So it is that in these days the Church may sometimes fail to meet desperate human needs, even in its own sphere of the care of persons as the cure of souls. We sometimes see a human situation like this. A person, eager to be helped in his distress, says, "I went to the Christian minister and he talked to me about God. It was very nice and very comforting; but he left me with my problem exactly as it was before. I went to some other professional man; he didn't talk to me about God, but he knew what he was talking about in terms of my personal problem and, through his help, the problem has largely been lifted." That kind of situation, when it occurs, is the outcome of a concept of the Church's relation to society which has dwelt on the primacy of God and religion in a way which does not relate that primacy to persons as they are amidst the turmoil of our contemporary life.

Second, in contrast, is another picture of the

church's role in society. It is the picture which has been made familiar in America, and to a lesser degree in England, by Harvey Cox's books, *The Secular City* and *God's Revolution and Man's Responsibility*. This view is far from being one of Christianity without God, for theology is prominent in these two books and the author seeks to draw his concepts from the Bible. But his theme is that God, who led His people out of Egypt and revealed to Moses His own new name, is today leading His people out into a new mode of knowing Him and serving Him. He is leading them out of the realm of religious culture, with its apartness and its spiritual exercises, into the realm of the secular city where God is disclosing Himself. Cox sees the secular city as the flowering of God's own purpose; within it Christians are to find God disclosing His own new name and calling them to serve Him in the down-to-earth tasks of human reconciliation and in the conserving of the values of personal life amidst situations where depersonalizing forces are so powerful. And the Church must shed religion and "do theology"; to "do theology" means to grapple with the problems of race, poverty, housing, underprivilege, wherever those problems are found.

Here is seen a new understanding of the sacraments: they are not the means of our incorporation into a community and life apart, but the means of our being plunged into the turmoil and the suffering of the world's life. Here too is a new understanding of the Church. It is, in Cox's presentation, a definite body of people with definite pledges, commitments, and discipline. But it is not a company of people gathered into a religious cultus so much as a number of cells of people thoroughly trained in the technical skills for grappling with life's problems, and disciplined to serve where they are most needed. Thus will the God of the Bible show Himself with a new name and in a new way if His people have the faith to leave behind almost all the old ideas of what the knowledge and the service of God involve.

You can drive out nature with a pitchfork, as the poet Horace said, but she goes on coming back. *Naturam expellas furca, tamen usque recurret.* So the religious dimension in life, inherent in the meaning of man himself, is bound to return. And sure enough Harvey Cox picks up the necessity of religion and abandons much of his former thesis in his latest book, *The Feast of Fools,* with its exciting insistence on the religious dimension in life. But the Achilles' heel of his former thesis is seen not in the issue of religion so much as in the issues of grace and redemption. While dwelling much on the reconciliation of man to man, he did no justice to the apostolic emphasis on the reconciliation of mankind to God. It is by the unmerited acts of divine forgiveness that men and women are freed to serve one another in humility and not in the pride and possessiveness which so easily beset philanthropy.

I have put in a stark contrast two pictures of the role of the Church towards society. The one so expresses the Church's Godward role as to miss the real world of persons in which the God-wardness is to be wrought out; the other so identifies the Church's role with the service of human problems as to fail to bring them into the eternal light of God. Is there a more excellent way?

I think it may be found in terms of the double aspect of the serving Church as *diakonos* and *doulos*. With that in mind we shall not solve every problem, but we are more likely to avoid false answers and to have a right grasp of the Church's mission. Thus, as *diakonos* the Church will throw itself into the service of the community in dis-interestedness and love. Its members will be eager in their witness in race relations, not by a patron-ising concern but by an identification with those who are underprivileged. Its members will be no less active among the poor and hungry, as being poor and hungry with them. Yet amidst its deep involvement in the service of the community the Church will keep alive for its own members, and strive to keep alive for others, three unchanging evangelical themes.

The first of these themes is the priority of *divine forgiveness* as providing the keynote of Christian ethics. Is not the concept of forgiveness all too often crowded out of the human scene? The word *forgive* is either not used at all or used in shallow ways. But the Christian community is the forgiven community; that is the ground of its relation to God and of the humility of its service of man.

The second theme is *heaven*. Do you feel that in our contemporary teaching and preaching there is not nearly enough emphasis upon heaven? Heaven is, after all, the goal of man's existence as a creature made in God's own image with the potentiality of enjoying the divine glory everlastingly. Heaven gives meaning to our existence now; defines the infinite worth of every man, woman, and child; and provides the perspective in which life's problems are seen. It is only a false idea of heaven which can be "escapist" or selfish, for love is one and indivisible and the love whose perfection is heaven is the same love which drives a man to forego comfort in the service of those who suffer.

The third theme is *worship*. It will be a worship that is not apart from the life of the world but set right in the heart of that life. The rage of activism can leave men and women starved in their power of contemplation; and in their starvation we see them turning to cults and techniques sometimes old and Eastern, and sometimes new-fangled and Western. The Church will find in the 'new spirituality' a practice of adoration and contemplation in the midst of the world's busyness, reproducing in our time the truth expounded in the *Letter to Diognetus* of old, "as the soul is in the body, so are the Christians in the world."

If such is the more excellent way, we can begin to see the respective roles within it of the laity and the ordained priesthood.

The laity, men and women, are increasingly coming into their rightful place in their share in liturgy, government, evangelism, practical witness. There is the service of the Christian layman within his own profession. There are the groups or cells of laymen who together worry out a problem of Christian behavior in the strength of the Gospel. There is the Christian congregation, acting collectively in its service of the community around it. There is a wider influence of Christian laymen within politics, civic or national. We thank God for the immense enhancement of the role of the laity in our time.

What then of the ordained priest? In the Churches in England and on the continent of Europe, far fewer men find themselves called to the ordained priesthood. Future historians will be better equipped to assess the causes of this than we ourselves can be at this moment. There is the pressure of secularism and irreligion. There is the half-conscious anticlericalism which is a by-product of the enhanced place of the laity. But there is also, amongst those who ardently desire to serve our Lord and His Church, often a genuine bewilderment about the significance of ordained priesthood in the modern world. There are young men with an eager sense of vocation who are yet unsure what the role of the priest means.

Now the traditional doctrine of the priest as minister of God's word and sacraments still stands, and the language of the New Testament about the unique role of the apostles is not outdated. Yet an empirical approach is needed, an approach which starts 'where people are' and sets the questions about the priesthood right in the context of those ideas that *are* grasped and understood.

The context therefore is the whole body of the

faithful, called to a royal priesthood of offering to God and service to mankind, with the privilege of sonship, than which none can be higher, and the varieties of ministry, which are all of Christ. Within that context what is the role and necessity of the clergy? They are men set apart for functions in a way that keeps the Church rooted in the Gospel of salvation.

First, the priest is one who learns theology and teaches it. His study is deep and constant, not that he may be erudite but that he may be simple. His teaching of theology is not done *de haut en bas* for, while he teaches the laity what they do not know without his help, he must all the while be learning from them about the questions to which theology is applied. In this partnership of priest and laity, the authority of the priest to teach in Christ's name is a real authority, but it will be exercised with the humility of Christ and in the spirit of one who learns.

Next, the priest represents in the life of the Church the dimension of a Divine Reconciliation. He will find himself but one of many agencies who help distressed souls with various skills and techniques. But amidst them all it will be for him to represent the often-forgotten dimension of God's forgiveness of the contrite. He will do this in absolution and in the preaching of God's reconciliation of the world once for all in the Cross of Christ.

So, too, the priest will be in a special way the Man of Prayer. True, all Christians are men and women of prayer, and there is no distinction in their access to the Father or in the power of their intercession. Yet the prayer of a priest is in a real way a focusing of the prayer of the Church to his teaching of theology and his office in absolution. The knowledge of God which is by books and brains is idle without the knowledge which prayer can bring. And as absolver the priest shares, on the one hand, in the broken heart of sin and penitence and, on the other hand, in the sorrow and joy of Christ who bears our sins and pardons them. The work of a pastor is a work of prayer with its own intensity of sorrow and joy.

Lastly, and in a way which sums up all, the priest is the Man of the Eucharist. Again, it is to all the faithful that the liturgy belongs; it is their sacrament, their offering, their breaking of the bread their showing of the Lord's death. The priest is among them, completely one with them. Yet he is more than their functional representative. By his role he represents the dependence of the sacrament upon the historic Gospel of Christ and upon the Church as a whole in its historic continuity. His office represents that dimension of the more than local, the more than contemporary, which is the true context of the rite in the Gospel and in the Church Catholic. He acts with Christ's authority, and his humility can show that he does so.

Slaves of Christ and servants of men. Can we recapture the truth and wonder of this vocation?

Ah, thou who tendest this poor vine,
tread out the grapes and all the wine
be theirs and thine.

3. *Toward Unity*

The word *reunion* is a poor word because it fails to represent the dynamic and many-dimensional theme of Christian unity as we find it in the seventeenth chapter of St. John and in the Epistle to the Ephesians. Let me recall briefly what these two great writings of the New Testament tell us about unity.

In John 17 we notice that unity is founded upon truth: "sanctify them in the truth; thy word is truth." It is a unity between the disciples and one another through their being "in" Christ and "in" the Father; their relationship with Christ is realised in holiness as Christ consecrates Himself, that they too may be consecrated. While unity is given once-for-all it is something into which the disciples will grow as a goal and a consummation: the Revised Standard Version of the Bible brings this out by its correct rendering in verse 23, "that they may *become* perfectly one." The goal is in part beyond the world and in heaven, when the disciples will come to the vision of the glory in which they already share; it is in part in history, where the world will come to believe as a result of the unity of the disciples.

In Ephesians amidst a different idiom and vocabulary the same themes are found. There is the emphasis upon holiness, expressed now in the growth of all the members of the Church into Christ's own manhood; there is the emphasis upon truth, now summed up as "one Lord, one faith, one baptism, one God and Father of all"; there is the emphasis upon future realization as gifts are given for the work of ministry "until we all attain to the unity of the faith and of the knowledge of the Son of God, to mature manhood . . . . " Two further themes, unmentioned in John 17, find emphasis in Ephesians. One is the specific inclusion of the new fellowship between Jews and Gentiles within the picture of human unity. The other is the cosmic range of the unity brought by Christ. Not only are all men to be united in Him, but "all things" (1:10) are to be so united. May we see in the phrase "all things" a depth of meaning which we may fail to understand but have no right to limit? The intractable forces in the world, whether we describe them in the mythological terms which St. Paul would use or in the terms of some of the modern sciences, are to be brought to serve the unity which Christ creates.

These Biblical themes are very familiar to us all. I would like, however, to draw out three aspects of them which are rightly recovering prominence at the present time. They are the relationship of unity and holiness, seen specially in the call to renewal in the life of the Church; the thought that unity though once given is always a goal towards which Christians move — call this, if you will, the eschatological or futuristic aspect of unity; and the unity of all men and all things in Christ, as ecumenism reaches out to the entire scene of human life and indeed to the physical environment in which the human race lives.

First: unity, holiness, renewal. To put this theme quite simply, our being with one another and in one another as Christians goes with our being with Christ and in Christ, and we may become closer to one another through being closer to Him. Let the Churches become more Christlike, let them serve Christ in a deeper and wider practical obedience, and the work of unity goes forward. Here Pope John XXIII had a prophetic influence both within and beyond the Church of Rome by linking the hope of the unity of all Christians with the renewal of all Christians in the obedience of Christ. Hence there was the strong emphasis of the Second Vatican Council upon the renewal of the Church. This was apparent in the pleas for a deeper spirituality, a more dynamic liturgical life, a fuller participation of the laity both in the liturgy and in evangelism, and new emphasis upon the use of the Holy Scriptures, not only as a source of doctrine but as the spiritual food of the faithful. No less important has been the new note of 'collegiality' in authority apparent in some of the Decrees of the Council. If the new role of collegiality is seen to be in conflict with other notes within the Church, its emergence has been of the utmost significance for Christendom.

Though its results have varied in different localities, the call to renewal has been influential far and wide within the Roman Catholic Church, and it has influenced parallel movements of renewal in other Communions. Genuine renewal 'in Christ' brings closer together those who know themselves to be 'in Christ.' Here we find a new way of looking at the problems of unity. In dialogue between Churches we find ourselves asking not, How can we unite our ecclesiastical structures just as they are, and our various Communions just as we now find them? but rather, How can our Church life be renewed, re-formed, or brought more effectively into the obedience of Christ? We find ourselves asking urgently, How can my own Church be better doing the will of Christ, in its form and organization, in its conduct of its affairs, in its mission, in its service of humanity, in its theology and teaching? This spiritual procedure throws the members of different Churches, Roman Catholic, Anglican, Protestant, more closely together in their effort to discover the divine will and to do it. The members of one Church often find the members of another Church wrestling with the same questions as themselves and sometimes finding the same answers. Sometimes this happens in matters where barriers had seemed most hard to overcome, like liturgy and sacramental doctrine; perspectives at once far older and far newer than those of the classic controversies come to be disclosed. Nothing is more heartening than to see Roman Catholics, Anglicans, and Christians of other communions sharing retreats together, studying the scriptures together, worshipping together and asking together, How can my own Church become more Christlike?

The second theme is unity as both given once for all in history and yet awaiting realization in the future. Once for all Christ gave to the Church the unity and the truth which are His. Yet through the centuries the Church is sent to grow into the perfect apprehension of the truth, and to realize perfectly a unity which is to be wrought out amidst diversity, of nations and cultures, and of temperaments and religions and intellectual experiences. The ecumenical task is never rightly to be described as if it were like the reconstruction of a toy once made in its completeness and subsequently broken. Had there been no quarrels in the Church of Corinth, no schisms in the Church, no great schisms between East and West, there would still be the growth through years of spiritual and intellectual struggle into the fullness of the unity which Christ once gave.

If this aspect of unity is borne in mind it is possible to combine a strong adherence to tradition with a generous recognition of what those who have deviated from tradition may yet, under God, bring to the unity of the future. I find this note prominent in a number of present-day Roman Catholic writers. I quote as an illustration some words by Father Yves Congar in his work *Chretiens en Dialogue,* published in Paris in 1964 and in an English translation in 1966:

> As Catholics, we must maintain genuine fidelity in the dogmatic affirmation of our Church that both unity and apostolicity have been granted to us in her. For us, fidelity to Catholic dogma is the truth. All the same, such fidelity can have two dimensions because Catholic truth itself has two dimensions in that it is a living truth, subject to development. There is a simple fidelity to the truth in the form it assumes at a given stage of its development, and also fidelity to the trend of that development in so far as it contains potentialities which have not at the moment been actualized.
>
> In the perspective of such a development, it can be admitted that the Church of eventual reunion will be in a position which has not yet been reached and lies before both us and our separated brethren. All that we believe is that this point will lie along the line of development of the Catholic Church and will thus belong to the continuity of the Church whose apostolicity dates from the day of Pentecost. At what precise stage in its development reunion will take place, to what degree of purification it will correspond, we do not know. . . . We can freely admit that if reunion does take place one day it will be *with a Church which differs in some ways* from the present condition of the Catholic Church, different because it will have developed and been purified and reformed in more than one respect through living contact with its deepest sources, particularly with holy scripture. . . .
>
> Ecumenism . . . does not consist directly in lead-

ing our separated brethren, either individually or
in groups, into confessional adherence to the
Catholic Church such as it is at the moment. To be
sure, no Catholic worthy of the name would refuse
to help a separated brother who, doubtful of the
truth of his own position, wished to become a
Catholic. Nevertheless, the ecumenical worker as
such feels himself impelled to work for unity at a
different level and in a different way. For him the
aim is to help other Christian communities and, if
one may so speak, his own Church also, to approach and converge upon the plenitude which
lies before us, in the light of which integration will
really be able to take place.

It is of little importance here to know whether
this point of convergence is eschatological or
belongs to history. The important thing is to work
for fruition of all that is Christian in the world. It is a
process in which the Catholic Church will continue
to reform and purify herself, to develop in herself,
and if need be to rediscover any values which are
hers but which, in her present state in time, she
does not integrally honor. The dissident communities, on their part, will also purify themselves,
correct their deviations . . . and pursue their evolution towards the totality of truth, converge upon
that point of plenitude to which the Catholic
Church may not have yet attained but which she
knows to lie along her own trajectory alone. [1]

I have quoted this passage at some length, not as
suggesting that Anglicans can accept all that it
says, but because it shows us a Roman Catholic
theologian adhering tenaciously to his own tradition and at the same time ascribing a very positive
significance to other communions and doing so in

virtue of his emphasis upon the Church as moving towards a future plenitude. Within the Decrees of the Second Vatican Council we see signs of a similar kind of thought. The Decree *De Ecumenismo* draws out the pilgrim attitude of the Church:

> Every renewal of the Church is essentially grounded in an increase of fidelity to her own calling. Undoubtedly this is the basis of the movement towards unity. Christ summons the Church to continual reformation as she goes on her pilgrim way (Ch. 5).

And it is this which enables a new relationship to separated Christians and communions:

> Nor should we forget anything wrought by the grace of the Holy Spirit in the hearts of our separated brethren can be a help towards our own edification (Ch. 4).

These theological considerations have greatly helped the growing fraternal relationships between Roman Catholics and Anglicans in so many parts of the world. But it is for us as Anglicans to apply these same principles *mutatis mutandis* in our relation to Christian communions which the course of history has separated from ourselves. I give one instance. In England the Anglican Church has been seeking union with the Methodists. How do we approach the problem? On the one hand we insist upon the preservation of certain norms of the Church's catholicity, once given and never to be abandoned, such as the Creeds, the tradition of episcopal ordination and the offices of bishop and presbyter as effectual signs of the givenness and historic continuity of the Church. But while we conserve these things and insist on their conservation within any union in which we share, we can know that our own understanding of these norms is very far from perfect, that our own use of them is no less far from perfect, and through union with others we shall learn not only what is true in *their* traditions but also the greater meaning of our own traditions, as together with those now separated from us we grow towards a future plenitude. Our attitude therefore can never be simply, "come back to Mother." Rather is it our calling to unite what Tillich called "the catholic substance" with the many Christian experiences which have grown somewhat apart from "the catholic substance." It helps in this process if, taught by John 17 and the Epistle to the Ephesians, we think of the unity of the Church as once given and as yet to be realized in a future plenitude.

Third, the unity for which our Lord prayed embraces aspects of human life more numerous than those which belong to the limited realm of ecclesiastical concerns. Through the unity of the *ecclesia* all people and all things are destined to become one in Christ.

There are today, not least amongst the younger people in the Church and on the fringe of the Church, many who are wearied by ecumenism as it often seems to be a movement enjoyed by ecclesiastics preoccupied with ecclesiastical problems. Let it be made clear that ecumenism includes every part of the healing of the wounds of races and nations. It is idle for, let us say, an

Episcopal Church and a Presbyterian Church to be planning union together if in either or in both of them there is the separation of race or color within the household of Christ. Every breaking down of barriers which divide humanity, social, racial, economic, cultural, is a part of the ecumenical task. The ecclesiastical aspects of ecumenism must be seen in this larger context. When they are so seen it is apparent that ecumenism is no hobby for church-minded people; it is a task of divine and human reconciliation in which every Christian man, woman, and child can have a share.

Furthermore Christ died and rose again in order to unite not only all people but all things. We are here on the fringe of a vast topic where our understanding is but small. But may there not be modern counterparts to St. Paul's mythological picture of the dethroning of demonic forces and the uniting of super-human powers? Man today seems in the grip of impersonal forces which thwart him at every turn. It is for man to use his growing powers over nature not for divisive selfishness but for brotherhood, mutual service and the glory of God. It is in this context that we see both the problem of those economic forces which make for the terrible contrast of affluence and hunger and the problem of man's pollution of the atmosphere of land, sea, and air in which he lives.

I have drawn out from two of our basic documents, the seventeenth chapter of St. John and the Epistle to the Ephesians, some aspects of Christian unity which seem to be pressing themselves upon the contemporary scene. I have not spoken today specifically of Anglican relations with the Church of Rome, with the Holy Orthodox Church, and with the Protestant Churches. Rather I have dwelt upon themes which bear upon every part of the ecumenical task: renewal in holiness, the Church's given unity and future plenitude, and the unity of all peoples and all things. This last theme has both its necessity and its danger. It is possible for us when we are frustrated in the field of ecclesiastical unions and unsure in the quest of holiness to clutch at social action and to turn ecumenism into a kind of one-dimensional activism. To do this is to be shallow, for while social action is a true part of ecumenism and a test of our Christianity, it is no substitute for the deep quest of unity in *truth* and *holiness* for which our Lord prayed. As the Church on earth dies to self in serving the Gospel of divine truth it is drawn nearer to the Church in heaven, which is the true country of those who are called to be saints.

**The Archbishop
of
Malines-Brussels :**

4. *The Church as Mission*

My dear Brethren and friends. First of all, I wish to thank you for your kind invitation to come here so that we can share together our common concerns about the Church; about the Church of today, of tomorrow, and of the future. It is a special joy for me to be engaged in this task with my good and dear friend, Archbishop Ramsey. Relations between Malines and Canterbury have known a cordial history ever since my predecessor, Cardinal Mercier, and Lord Halifax began the famous "Conversations" in 1921. I think Lord Halifax and Cardinal Mercier must be smiling on us this evening.

It was said this morning, and it is very true, that we are living in difficult times. Yes, these are difficult times, but they are also hopeful ones. One of the principal factors that make these times so difficult is the fact that the world is evolving so rapidly that it requires every effort to stay abreast of the pace. Someone remarked that, according to former measures of time, every ten years brings a century of change, and perhaps before long the figure will be every five years; for even our process of evolution is evolving rapidly. I remember the Rector of my seminary saying to me before I went to see a group of young seminarians, "I feel I must tell you that the students of today are living in another world than we did." A few days later, he said to me, "I think I was mistaken. These students are not living in another sort of world — they are on another planet." And I believe that is true.

We are living, then, in an evolving world, and at the same time in an evolving Church. But that is as it should be since the Church should be evolving in an evolving world. It is the very nature of the Church to be a Church on the road, a Pilgrim Church, a Church coming from the past being present today on its way toward a future where there will be a meeting with Christ at the end of time. Evolution, movement, direction toward the future — these are the essential characteristics of the Church, which believes and lives and loves in the total dimension of hope. Pope John said one day laughingly, "You know they speak of me as a transition Pope. That is true but the continuity of the Church is made from transition to transition."

Thus the difficulty that faces us, and I suppose that in this regard our problems are very similar, yours and mine, is that we have in one and the same Church many different views regarding the role of transition in the Church and the effect of modern rapid change on the life of the Church. In the Roman Catholic terminology I would say that we have people of a 'Vatican I' mentality, others of 'Vatican II' mentality, others still, of a 'Vatican III' mentality, and it is no small task to keep all these together working and sacrificing to preserve unity. Any leader in the Church is inevitably exposed to criticism: he is going too slowly for 'Vatican III' and too fast for 'Vatican I.' At times the tension can be very great. There are some who say, "We must keep both feet on the ground and be truly conservative." Others answer them, "But, if you keep your two feet on the ground nothing will happen; we must go forward." And they put both feet in the air. No, we must walk, we are on pilgrimage, and he who walks has one foot on the ground and one foot in the air; that is progress. It is the role of prudence to take the right risks, lifting a foot at the proper time, placing a foot in the right direction. Fear would like to keep both feet immobile; impatience, and sometimes another kind of fear, would like to try to jump with both feet in the air. Optimism knows how to walk.

And so it is true, these are difficult times; but they are also hopeful times. It is precisely because the changes are so profound and are touching upon the very roots of our existence, that things can happen today, which yesterday were impossible. Day by day I experience the surprises of the Holy Spirit. I believe that the Spirit of God can surprise us: I have confidence in statistics, but only to a limited degree, and I have respect for sociological data, but always with the knowledge that the Spirit of God can break through the deter-

minism created or predicted on a human level and
burst forth in a sunshine of surprises. You are all
familiar with the saying, "The difficult you can do
at once; the impossible needs a bit more time."
Well, I think really, we are living in an age in
which many impossibilities are becoming possible; for instance, the fact that I am here.

As you know, I have been invited to speak about
the future of the Church. I gave some thought to a
plan for these talks and when I had finished my
own plannng, I asked Dr. Ramsey, "What is your
plan?" His was exactly the same. So I will speak
now about the Church and the Spirit of faith,
under the specific aspect of the Church as a
mission to the world, the Church as coming from
God and going through the world, going to men.
Tomorrow I will speak about the Church as a
service to man. These two aspects represent the
rhythm or economy of salvation; they are its two
movements. The Church is Christ among us today;
Christ living today; redeeming and sanctifying
humanity today through His Spirit. Christ is the
Mediator and so the Church is nothing else than
Christ, living in us now and through us performing
that same work of mediation, bringing God and
man together; establishing God and man in communion. The effecting of this reconciliation can be
viewed in either of two ways: as it starts from God
through Christ to man, or as it begins from men,
where they are, through Jesus Christ to God.
Under the first aspect, the Church is considered as
a mission, coming out of the Heart of the Father,
giving us Christ and the Holy Spirit for the world

and the men of today. This evening we will consider this aspect, and tomorrow we will consider its correlative. We are faced with the same problem as that which faced the builders of the tunnel of St. Gotthard in Switzerland: you can start from the Italian side or the Swiss side; the main point is that the two efforts be joined and that the tunnel be complete. The danger in approaching from either side is that the effort will never reach its destinaton.

If we wish to foster dialogue between the Church and the World, if we wish to share in the reality of the Church as a mission to the world, then in all truthfulness before the Lord, we should ask ourselves what we mean when we say 'Church', or rather, What does God mean in creating this mysterious reality the Church and preserving it in the world? I think the whole answer to this question must begin with these words of the Lord; "As the Father sent Me, so am I sending You" (John 20:21). The Church is the continuing of Christ's mission; it is the extension, in space and time, of the Father's sending of the Son as His own gift to the world. There is the essence of the Church. It was never by some sort of decision made one day in the past that the Church decided to be missionary. No, the Church is missionary by its very nature. It continues and extends the apostolic community instituted by Christ to bear the message to every creature. The Church sprang from the Word of God and is at the service of that Word. She is the new Israel carrying

on and fulfilling the mission of the Chosen People
for the salvation of the whole world. The Biblical
concept of election is not synonymous with sine-
cure; it is inseparable from the notion of mission
and ministry. That is to say, the Divine election,
while creating a special intimacy with God, implies
the idea of a vocation, of a call, and consequently
of responsibility before God. By faith and baptism
the Christian becomes a member of the apostolic
community and, as such, he enters into the intentions of God for the world. He is called to open
his heart to the salvific will of God with regard to
sinful humanity; for this reason, his prayer must be
henceforth, "Thy Kingdom come, Thy Will be
done." In brief, to belong to the Church of Christ
is at once a grace and a responsibility; it implies
for every Christian the duty of collaborating toward the building up of the Church in both senses
of the word "edify."

The Church is by essence missionary. We can
also say that it is missionary by a very solemn
command of the Lord. At the moment our Blessed
Lord was leaving the earth He gave His Apostles
this solemn command: "All authority in heaven
and on earth has been given to me. Go, therefore,
make disciples of all the nations; baptise them in
the name of the Father and of the Son and of the
Holy Spirit, and teach them to observe all the
commands I gave you. And know that I am with
you always; yes, to the end of time" (Matthew
28:18-20). I think that from time to time we have to
read these sacred words as though we were
listening to them for the first time. "All *dynamis,*

all power, all authority is given to *Me*," and "*I* will be with you." We must connect these two statements of the Lord. All of us know what obstacles face us today, but we are to realize first of all, not the magnitude of the obstacles, but the fact that in Christ there is all power — and He is with us. We are often tempted to raise the same question the women did on the way to the Easter tomb: "Who will remove the stone from the door of the tomb?" But the Lord is risen! He is here and His command is, "Go, and bring the Gospel to every creature" (Mark 16:15).

We are sent to everyone without exception. I remember a parish priest saying to me, "But how can I go and visit twenty thousand parishioners? It is impossible." I answered, "Well, the command of the Lord is, 'Go, and bring the Gospel to every creature.' The solution must be found; you have to find it. The Lord didn't say, and I, your Bishop, don't say to you, Go and visit those twenty thousand parishioners yourself, but still, you are responsible that they be visited and that the Gospel be brought to them. This is your apostolic and pastoral duty. You must find ways of acting in full coresponsibility with all the Christians around you so that the Gospel is brought to everyone in your parish." We have to make these efforts and not allow our enthusiasm to ebb and flow with the tide of success. I remember having read the answer of a missionary in China who, before he was a priest, was a very successful layman. Someone said to him that it was a shame for him to have spent so many years as a missionary in China without any visible success. He answered, "I am not here because of any past or future successes but to obey the command of the Master and bring the Gospel to every creature." That is, I think, an expression in faith of what our mission is: we go because the Lord said, "Go," because Christ wishes to go, in and through us. He has told us to go and preach the Gospel and, by that, He means all of the Gospel; every page and every verse. Our duty is not satisfied when we have only sketched out the main lines of the Gospel — no, we must make Christ present, for the Gospel is Jesus; it is He whom we are meant to preach in all the reality, power, and attractive beauty of His being, so that all men hear within themselves the echo of the full implications of His call to holiness and union with the Father; we must go bearing this Gospel to every creature to the end of the world.

This mystery and this urgency were well understood by the saints. Saint Francis said to his brothers: "Preach, using words if you are able. But above all preach with your lives and deeds." And Charles de Foucauld wrote: "People should be able to see by looking at the brothers and sisters . . . what the Gospel is, what Jesus is . . . . They should themselves be a living Gospel."

So, if the Church is a missionary reality by essence and by command of the Lord, it is most important that every Christian understand this if he is to understand himself. I am not familiar with the Anglican experience in this regard, but I must admit that, among Roman Catholics, it is extremely difficult to convince the average lay person that the missionary task of the Church was not confided to bishops and priests as an exclusive prerogative, but that it pertains to all Christians as a result of their baptism. A baptised man is an apostle or he is not fully baptised. I remember at the beginning of the Council someone asked me, "In your opinion, what is the number one problem facing Vatican II?" I answered, "As I see it, the number one problem is, how to change passive Christians into active Christians, so that they take seriously the command of the Lord, expressing the very nature of their individual and communal reality by obeying His injunction to 'Go, and bring the Gospel to every creature.' "

In our Belgian catechism one of the first questions that is posed is this: "Why were you created?" Well, in Belgium we are created — according to our catechism — "To know God, to love God, to serve God, and in that way to save our soul." But that is only half the reality. Actually, we are created to know God and to *make Him known,* love God and to *make Him loved;* to serve God, and to *make Him served."* Otherwise we are just half Christians. A Christian man is someone to whom Christ has confided responsibility for other men. Irresponsibility means non-Christianity; Christian means responsible. Vatican II has reminded us that Christian holiness is the fullness of being human, and as Antoine de Saint Exupery once said, "To be a man is, precisely, to be responsible. It is to feel shame at the sight of what seems to be unmerited misery. It is to take pride in a victory won by one's comrades. It is to feel, when setting one's stone, that one is contributing to the building of the world." [2]

Our duty, then, is to bear the Good News to all the world. Even if this were not of the very essence of the Church and enjoined upon us by the command of the Lord, we would still be obliged to be missionaries, just to keep the faith. There is no other way to keep the faith. I remember some years ago the Bishops of England came together to study the problems of the Irish faithful coming over to England and subsequently losing their faith. Many analyses were undertaken, many remedies proposed, until finally at one of the meetings of Irish Bishops, Frank Duff, a very holy man and the founder of the Legion of Mary, was invited to give his opinion and advice. That man of faith gave this answer: "Teach the faithful to spread the faith, to give it — if you wish to keep the faith, you have to give it." That is the inner secret, I think, of our Lord's command. As we obey Christ and seek to spread the faith, our own faith deepens and our own preaching becomes more permeated by the Holy Spirit. "Anyone who finds his life shall lose it; anyone who loses his life for my sake will find it" (Matthew 10:39). This means that we have to tell our people that the Christian man is someone in whom our Saviour is acting today, speaking today, going to others today. At this moment Christ has no other tongue to speak on earth but our tongue; no other feet to walk on earth, but our feet.

And so, as we see, our Lord did not say to everyone, "Go and be a great preacher," but rather, "Announce the Good News." We have to do what we can: we must express our faith according to circumstances, we must "preach the Gospel with our lives." All Christians, all members of the Church, all the members of God's people must be convinced of their dignity and responsibility in this regard. We just read the Gospel that told us of the small boy who had five barley loaves and two fish. What he offered is completely out of proportion to the needs of the people gathered before our Lord: "What are these, among so many?" (John 6:10). Yet, Christ was waiting for just that gesture, that insignificant offer, in order to exercise His power and feed all those who were hungry. Sometimes it is only necessary that we take the risk of speaking but a single word, offering a tiny gesture or a smile, as our contribution to bearing the Good News, and the Father uses this to heal, console, and strengthen. We offer what little we can and are surprised to find that it is an important instrument of grace. A preacher, who one day had converted someone by his sermon, asked the man, "Could you tell me what part of my sermon really convinced you?" The man replied, "O Father, I will never forget that one point in your sermon when you said, 'Brethren, I have finished the first part of my sermon and will now start the second part.' Well, that struck me very strongly and I said to myself, 'Dear boy, you have to finish the first part of your life and start a new part.'" We never know what instruments our Lord will use.

A few weeks ago I had the joy of meeting one of

your theologians in Malines. He has just written a very interesting book about the Eucharist in which we can find these sentences: "To hear God's Word is to be transformed by the Word . . . . Any truly Christian word, even though only spoken, has power to change a person, for as a Christian word it is God's expression of himself; it is God influencing our lives through personal dialogue with us. Since God is personal power and the Word is God, truly to hear the Word enables God to be present with power to the hearer. To hear God's Word is an event in one's life, the event of being with God." [3]

So far I have spoken about our obligation to be ourselves, that is, to assume responsibility as Church for our missionary reality and to obey the command of the Lord to bring the Good News to everyone. This has never been an easy task, but today the obstacles to our missionary self-realization are particularly difficult and loom especially large. In speaking this way, I do not feel there is any need for me to make a distinction between Roman Catholicism and the Anglican Church; these obstacles confront us equally and it is as brothers that we search for their solution.

There is a prevailing tendency to question missionary activity and missionary responsibility: many people, laity and ministers of the Gospel alike, are questioning the Church's role in proclaiming the Gospel in and to the world today. Their difficulties can be summed up, I think, in these three questions:

"Why should we go and preach today?"

"What are we to say with certitude today?"

"How can we give the message to the people of today?"

Let us consider these questions one by one.

Why should we go and preach today? When people ask this question, they are thinking of non-Christians throughout the world, both those who are in countries historically considered Christian and those who live in what used to be termed 'missionary lands.' Their questions, which can be found in the newspapers, theological reviews, interviews, etcetera, can be grouped around four main topics.

The *first* reason often invoked against approaching non-Christians with the message of the Gospel is the fact of liberty of conscience. "We have to respect the freedom of every individual's conscience; we have no right to go and impose our Christian Gospel upon anyone." I am speaking here in America, the country whose tradition has always fostered freedom and religious liberty. I really think that it was at this point in the Council's discussions that the American bishops played their most effective role. We have learned to respect freedom of conscience, and we must admit that we were not always without sin in this regard. History presents us with many sad examples of the message of Christian freedom being imposed by force upon people who neither understood nor as yet desired to accept the message of the Gospel. Such constraint is the very contradiction of the reality it purports to confer.

However, there is a vast gamut of possibilities between imposing the Gospel by physical or sociological force and never speaking of the Gospel under the pretext of respecting liberty of conscience; our Lord's command did not include the phrase, "Preach the Gospel until the twentieth century." He never said, "Force people to be converts," but rather, "Offer the Good News in a spirit of freedom and joy, and make it possible for everyone to accept it in the same spirit."

Whenever we possess any treasure that brings us joy, we express in a spontaneous gesture our desire to share it with others. When beholding a beautiful sunrise I say to someone, "Look, there is the dawn." I am not constraining him to raise his eyes, nor forcing him to view the dawn exactly as I do; I am offering my brother a deeper experience of joy. It isn't a question of proselytising, which is a bad word, or of high-pressure convert-making, but rather of allowing Christ, in and through me, to speak to another. The degree to which the other knows and accepts Christ's message is a mystery hidden in that secret encounter between God's grace and the other's freedom. To deny someone a chance of knowing the deepest source of my joy, is to respect neither his conscience nor mine.

The *second* reason offered very often as a motive for questioning the validity of missionary activity is that all religions are of value. "Everyone can be saved in his own religion. Why should we go and impose our religion on others?" First of all, it is not a question of being saved; secondly, it is a

question of obedience to the command of the
Lord, the depth of whose mysterious designs upon
the human race are beyond our dim powers of
understanding. Preaching the Gospel is not teaching a doctrine, but making the power of the
resurrection present. We are continuing the mission of the Word and this means, for us, that we
must learn the riches of the Word already present
in other cultures, in order to bring the riches
which God has "showered on us in all Wisdom
and insight, making known to us the mystery of
His purpose" (Ephesians 1:8-9).

Often our missionary activity has been too
European. We have been too dazzled by our own
achievements, too ready to identify European
ways with the message of the Gospel. We have
spoken much, but listened little. I was glad to hear
His Grace say this morning that we have a lot to
learn from Oriental religions. Up to this point, we
have understood them very badly, and this is true
also of the values to be found in African cultures,
as well as in others. It was the famous Anglican
missionary, Roland Allen, many of whose insights
are still valid today, who once wrote a book under
the provocative title, *Missionary Methods — St.
Paul's or Ours?* We should approach non-Christians being all things to all men and having St.
Paul's liberty to be "indebted to Greek and non-
Greek, to learned and simple" (Romans 1:14).
Then we could address our brothers, not as
though they possessed nothing, but in the Spirit of
our Lord and, aware of His presence within us, we
could say, "I come to you, so that you can have

life, and have it more abundantly." We are not coming to bring life to the dead, but an enrichment, a supplement of life to those already alive to many facets of the Gospel message.

The *third* reason often alleged as an obstacle to the preaching of the Gospel is the presence of social injustice. "Why go and preach the Kingdom of Heaven to those for whom life on earth is already a hell? Wait, solve the social problems first and then go and preach the gospel. Go and preach social revolution; work to bring about human justice; enter into the fight; and then, someday perhaps, you may have the right to speak." This is not a negligible objection, and tomorrow we shall have occasion to consider all the social implications of the Gospel, without which it is simply not Gospel; but we must remember the unifying center of this evangelical message. Underlying and unifying all the social, familial and national duties there is the presence of the Living Christ proclaiming and conferring a liberty in love beyond man's power to imagine. As Fr. M. D. Chenu once wrote, "Evangelization and civilization are in different orders. To feed men is, in itself, not to save them, even when my salvation demands that I feed them." We have to be very attentive to this distinction.

And there is a *final* reason often given as an obstacle to our preaching of the Gospel. It is pitiful to hear priests saying: "Why should we go to speak? Nobody is listening to us; the world is not ready to listen to us; mankind is not ready." I would answer, do you think that in the time of our

Lord, the Jews of Palestine were ready to hear and
to listen? I don't think so; you have only to look at
a Crucifix to realize that they were not ready. Do
you think that the intellectuals of Athens were
ready to hear Paul preaching about Resurrection?
I hardly think so. "When they heard about the
raising of the dead, some scoffed; and others said,
'We will hear you on this subject some other
time' " (Acts 17:32-33). Christ and His Apostles
addressed audiences which were not "ready." The
poignant thing today in the Christian world is not
that the non-Christian world is unprepared to
listen, it is that we are not ready to speak. This is
very important; there is some sort of mute devil
we have to exorcise. We have to pray once again
for an outpouring of the Holy Spirit which will
confer upon us, as He did upon the Apostles at
Pentecost, the gift of "bold speech" (see Acts 4:31).
Today we are tempted to invert St. Paul's citation
of Psalm 116, "I believed, and therefore I spoke"
(II Corinthians 4:13). We seem to be more prone
to translate it, "I believed, and therefore I re-
mained silent." May the Spirit confer upon us the
grace He gave to Paul so that we too "will have
none of the reticence of those who are ashamed,
no deceitfulness or watering down the Word of
God; but the way we commend ourselves to every
human being with a conscience is by stating the
truth openly in the sight of God" (II Corinthians
4:2).

What can we say with certitude today? It seems
that today everything is under question: the very

content of the faith is being placed under a cloud
of doubt. Karl Barth used to say, "Our Blessed
Lord said, 'Go, and bring my Word to everyone'
and the theologians of today have interpreted that
to mean, 'Go, and make a problem out of every
word I said." This morning His Grace spoke well
about the false security of theology. I think we
need theology, but theology is not to be confused
with faith. Faith is something coming directly from
the Living God to a living person; it is a living
dialogue between God, the living God, speaking
to a living man who hears and answers in a living
response. Our confidence is in the God of Life and
not in our powers of thought. Of course, we need
people thinking about the contents of our faith
and presenting it in new ways, but I think, in my
generation at least, we were much too preoccupied with knowing things with certitude.
Today we are more authentically searching for
understanding; that is progress. We don't know as
much about God today as we knew twenty-five
years ago.

Revelation is not a set of propositions, each
bearing its distinctive label of certitude defining
the limits of its discussion. No, faith is an encounter; faith is God meeting me, and my meeting
with God in prayer and contemplation. The first
letter of John contains a great challenge and at
times a great indictment of theology professors:
"Anyone who fails to love can never have known
God, because God is Love" (I John 4:8). That
means that if a professor of theology is not at the
same time both a sort of a contemplative and a

man striving for sanctity, his doctrine inspires no
confidence. In the tradition of the Eastern Church
this is brought out by such sayings as this one of
Evagrius: "If you really pray, you are a theologian,
and if you are a theologian, you really pray" *(De
Oratione,* 60). Or this one of St. Macarios: "A
theologian is a man who has been taught by God."
So let us pray for the holiness of our theologians. I
think that the movement we see about us today,
all the discussion about the death of God, is a
grace for the Church, because it has purified us
from too human a way of thinking and speaking
about God. That sort of God is, happily, dead.
When I came into the room a few minutes ago, I
noticed on the desk here a little sign; it read, "My
God is alive, Sorry about yours."

*What message can we bring to the men of
today?* The problem contained in this question is
not a small one, but it certainly is not insur-
mountable. It is basically the problem of relevance
within the phenomenon of change. We must
present the living faith, the fulness of the apostolic
tradition, to the men of today, and this means we
have to change our vocabulary. We have to
change because words are living realities and the
meanings of words change. It may be that to be
faithful to a reality I must express it in a radically
different, and perhaps in an opposite, way from
that in which it has been expressed before. If I
were to preach in China, instead of in Belgium, I
would say that Christ is sitting at the left hand of
the Father, not at the right, for in China the left

hand is the place of honor. When we present the mysteries of faith, we must be attentive to the cultural, conceptual, and sociological milieu in which the Word is being presented. We have to translate the message, and not only translate, but transpose into a different key, the harmonics of the Living Word. If the Message was first given in a rural setting, now we must change many of its images so that it truly speaks to people living in big cities, whose daily experience is of the urban reality. We must accept a healthy pluralism of philosophies and theologies, because what we have to say is so rich that it fills and transcends all its true expressions. We must strive to make our approximations more adequate, while bearing in mind that the highest degree of the knowledge of God is "to understand that one cannot understand Him" (St. Gregory of Nyssa).

And so to those who preach the Gospel today and feel at a loss as to what to say, I would counsel: don't be too impressed by the phenomenon of 'contemporary man.' He is not as completely unique as he sometimes likes to think he is. Allow yourself to experience the abiding problems of existence and to experience your faith in relation to those problems. There is something permanent in man and in mankind. Anyone, as long as he is truly man, cannot escape such questions as, "Why am I here?" "What is the meaning of life?" "What is the meaning of suffering?" "What is the meaning of Death?" "What is tomorrow?" All these questions are there, living in every soul, and we must be convinced that when we are speaking and bringing the Gospel we are answering an echo already existing in the people listening to us. Just a few days ago, I read these lines in Carl Jung's *Modern Man in Search of a Soul:* "During the past thirty years people from all the civilized countries of the earth have consulted me. I have treated many hundreds of patients . . . among all my patients in the second half of life — that is over thirty-five — there has not been one whose problem in the last resort was not that of finding a religious outlook on life."[4] This is the finding of a psychiatrist speaking from vast experience and profound reflection. When we are free enough to experience our own problems in their depths as contemporary men, and know the healing power of the Gospel in our own beings, we will not doubt its relevance for our brothers.

And so, just to end these reflections today, let us recall for our own encouragement, and that of the people for whom we are responsible, that the Church is by her nature a mission to the man of today in obedience to the perennial command of the Lord: He will never fail to give us what we need to be faithful to Him and to ourselves. I wish to add just one word: let us not forget that Mission means Redemption. Since the Church is Mission, and since the Mission of the Church is to continue the redeeming activity of the Lord, it is completely normal that it should know a Good Friday, that there should be suffering and even death. The Mission we have to accomplish is not a sort of human propaganda; it is making present the redemption in all its reality and consequences: this means the suffering of the Cross in the power of the Resurrection. "Wherever we go, we carry death with us in our body, the death that Jesus died, that in this body also life may reveal itself, the life that Jesus lives. For continually, while still alive, we are being surrendered into the hands of death, for Jesus' sake, so that the life of Jesus also may be revealed in this mortal body of ours" (II Corinthians 4:10-11).

5. *Christ, the Church, and the World*

It seems to me that the best way to understand the relationship between the Church and the world is to look first at the relationship between Christ and the world. The Church is, as we know, the sacramental presence of Christ on this globe. If we meditate, therefore, on the relationship between Christ and human reality, we will be able to situate the Church within the same context.

The relationship between Christ and the world can be summed up under three different headings or propositional expressions: Christ is in and for the world; Christ is against the world; and Christ is beyond the world.

Christ is in and for the world because He is the heart of the world; the living, life-center which gives reality its subsistence and direction. In the letter to the Colossians, St. Paul, quoting an ancient hymn, speaks of Christ as the "Image of the

unseen God, the first-born of all creation; for in
him were created all things in heaven and on earth
. . . all things were created through him and for
him. Before anything was created, he existed and
he holds all things in unity. For the Church is his
Body and he is its Head" (Colossians 1:15-18).
Exegetes point out to us that in this and in similar
passages, the New Testament is speaking of Christ,
the Word of God presiding at creation, and there
is no distinction between Word and Incarnate
Word since, as is clear from the prologue to St.
John's Gospel, the incarnation is the final dis-
tillation of the physical presence of the Word in
creation, a presence begun "In the beginning"
and gradually made more intense until "the Word
became flesh." Christ is the fulfillment of all
creation; He is the *Pantokrator*. In Christ there is
realized completely the vocation of Adam: Man
crowned with glory and honor and ruling the
whole world (see Hebrews 2:5-9).

Thus, Christ is present in the world outside the
physical limits of the Church. It is very important, I
think, to stress that there is only one world with
Christ at the heart and center of it. There are not
two worlds, one natural and the other super-
natural. The "natural order" is a convenient theological hypothesis, which can help us understand
reality as it is, but reality has been created *in
Christ*. The only existing world is a world in which
we are created, redeemed, and sanctified in Jesus
Christ. Creation, as such, is not a profane reality; it
is a Christian reality whose true dimensions lie
open to the gaze of faith.

But I would go a step further: Christ is presiding at creation, but creation is not a static thing accomplished once and for all; it is a dynamic process still on the way to completion. It might be true to say that "all the world's a stage," but then we must also bear in mind that this metaphor neglects another dimension of human existence: namely, that man in his bodily and social reality is himself the stage and that his every act modifies the reality experienced by himself and his brothers. The Scriptures suggest to us that creation is a dynamic act of a dynamic God, whch will only be completed at the end of the world. Scholars have noted that the latter chapters of the Book of Isaiah continually describe the act of creation by using a Hebrew active participle: God *is creating.* "Thus says God, Yahweh, he who is creating the heavens and spreading them out, who is giving shape to the earth and what comes from it, who is giving breath to its people and life to the creatures that move in it" (Isaiah 42:5).

Our concept of nature has been taken from the Greeks and applied to creation; that explains why it is too static. The Bible has an historical vision of creation. I have always found very attractive that phrase of Gabriel Marcel in which he says that "Human life is like a sentence which cannot be understood until the final word is spoken."

The creation of man in the image of God means that man is himself a creator. He collaborates in creation: it is in him but not without him that God's intentions become fully realized within creation. Past, present, and future are the time dimensions of one continuous, dynamic act still in the process of being realized.

But I would go even further: in Christ the world has not only been created but recreated. St. Gregory Nazienzen, in a famous Christmas sermon, described the nativity of Christ as a "festival of recreation." The birth of Christ, although an historical event, is not an end, but a means to the renewal, sanctification, and recreation of the whole universe. We commemorate not so much the birth of a child as the ultimate transfiguration of man and the whole created world.

> Christ redeemed humanity, and by taking humanity to Himself, He redeemed the world. When the Word of God was made flesh, He not only became the head of a new race, He became the Lord of a new creation. Christ in His flesh took the whole of creation into Himself, that it might share anew in divinity. In Christ the universe was radically transformed. In His person the world was consecrated and sacramentalized. Earth was redeemed, recreated. And while it is true to say that Christ in the past redeemed humanity, and by (redeeming) humanity he redeemed the world, it is equally true to say, in the peesent, that Christ redeems humanity and by humanity redeems the world. Objectively men were redeemed, but in another sense that was only the beginning of a new world, even until now the whole world is one great yearning cry, Creation's unceasing call for Redemption. [5]

In the Byzantine liturgical tradition, this same view of Christmas is echoed over and over again. In hymns and prayers the joy and wonder of creation and restoration become the theme around which other aspects of the nativity are gathered.

> Your Nativity, O Christ, our God, has shone the light of knowledge upon the world. Through it those who had been star-worshippers learned through a star to worship You, O Sun of Justice, and to recognize in You the One who rises and who comes from on high — O Lord, glory to You.
>
> Your coming, O Christ, has shed upon us a great light, O you Light of Light and Radiance of the Father! You have illumined the whole creation . . . .
>
> ——*Kontakion of Christmas*

> O Christ, what shall we offer you today
> For Your coming on earth as a man for our sake?
> Every creature that has its being from You gives
>   thanks to You:
> The angels offer You hymns of praise;
> The heavens give You a star;
> Wise men present their gifts
> And the shepherds their wonder;
> The earth provides a cave and the wilderness a
>   manger.
> As for us, we offer You a Mother, a virgin Mother.
> O God, who are from all eternity, have mercy on
>   us.
>
> ——*Matins of Christmas*

The presence of Christ in and for the world is one dimension of His relationship to it. Christ is also against the world and this aspect of the relationship points up the ambiguity introduced into creation by the sin of man. Christ came to save and redeem sinful humanity. His life and death were a battle against sin and the forces of sin: this is the meaning of His struggle and temptation at the beginning of His public life and at the crisis He experienced in the garden of Gethsemane. Today, after centuries of fearful animosity toward the world, we are very conscious of the meek Christ, the human Christ, the Christ who is moving the whole creation toward its completion; but we cannot afford to ignore the Christ who entered into combat with the demonic forces of physical suffering, alienation, abuse of power, and human malice. The victory of Christ over the forces that held His brothers in subjection was a victory that cost something. "Since all the children share the same blood and flesh, he too shared equally in it, so that by his death he could take away all the power of the devil, who had power over death, and set free all those who had been held in slavery all their lives by the fear of death" (Hebrews 2: 14-15).

But there is another aspect of Christ which I wish to stress today, namely, the fact that Christ is *beyond* the world. Christ came for us and for our salvation and if we see in Christ His complete dedication to man we must also see His most intimate dedication: the supreme love He has for His Father. He came into the world for us, yes, but that coming accomplished the will of the Father. He came to tell us about His Father and to teach mankind to address God as *Father*. As He left the upper room on His way to His passion, He declared, "The world must be brought to know that I love the Father and that I am doing exactly what

the Father told me. Come now, let us go" (John
14:31).

It is precisely love for and obedience to His
Father that makes of His redeeming death a life-
giving revelation of the Father. "What proves that
God [the Father] loves us is that Christ died for us
while we were still sinners" (Romans 5:8). It is
precisely the transcendent love of Christ for His
Father that is the unifying and life-giving power of
His presence in the world, against the unreality of
what we have done to the world. If we forget that
Christ is beyond the dimensions we prescribe for
reality, then we never touch upon that folly of
God that is wiser than all our reasoning and that
gives to existence meaning and beauty by carrying
it beyond itself.

In continuing to make Christ present, the
Church must be faithful to all three of the relations Christ has to the world. For the Church has
the task of continuing to reconcile man to God, to
bring man and God together in intimate communion. The Church must be a mediator by letting
Christ, in her, continue His mediating action. As I
said yesterday, we can view this activity in two
ways: we can consider God's initiative, the movement from God to man; that was the perspective
we had yesterday when we spoke of the Church as
Mission. Now we can consider the other movement, which begins from man and goes to God
through Jesus Christ. But before we begin this
consideration, we should reflect for a moment
and make, as it were, an examination of con-

science. Was the God from whom we considered
the movement to originate really the Living God,
and the man to whom we brought the Gospel —
was it really a living man? Was it man in the vibrant
complexity of his actual and daily existence? If we
reflect for a moment about the 'classical' God, the
God of the nineteenth century, it is easy to see
that the God we used to speak about was the God
of the philosophers and not the Father of our Lord
Jesus Christ. We had that God too easily under
control and too well categorized in our concepts.
Voltaire was quite justified in his quip about God
having made man in his image and man having
returned the compliment. The God we spoke
about was an oversimplified explanation of the
reality with which we were comfortable. Just think
about the way people sometimes speak about the
providence of God: during the war many times I
heard expressions like, "Oh, providence was
good, the bombs fell but they didn't hit my house,
they fell right next door." But the same God has to
be providence for everyone. The suffering that we
or others experience may create anguish of spirit,
but we cannot find peace by taking refuge in a
simplistic illusion. Teilard de Chardin once wrote,
"Whatever may be said, our century is religious,
probably more religious than any other; for how
could it fail to be, with such a vast horizon before
it and with such problems to be solved?" And then
he added this phrase, "The only thing is that —
our century has not the god it can adore." [6] We
Christians who "see the glory of God shining in
the face of Jesus" must bring this knowledge of
the living God to those who search for Him.

But then, there is also the other side to our question: this man to whom we were bringing God — was he really a living man in the full human sense of the word *life?* I think we have to answer No. We considered Christians as a religious people much too often in the narrow sense that equates 'religious' with 'church-going.' The Christian we addressed was the Sunday Catholic or Anglican or anything else. We only considered our fellow Christians in the light of our own clerical preoccupations; we addressed them in terms that we considered to be 'spiritual.' I remember as a student reading a wonderful and very helpful book; it was Dom Marmion's *Christ, the Life of the Soul.* It is still a good book but we would never give it that title today. Christ is not only the life of the soul; He is the life of man.

The Church has always had some difficulty in living close to life in all the richness of its concrete reality. That is because life always means evolution, change, and dynamic movement, and the Church, humanly speaking — and this is especially true of the hierarchy — is afraid of change. We bishops seem always to be on the defensive, we find it almost impossible to swim with the current, even when that current is being moved by the Spirit of God. We have only to look at our history, remote and recent, to see how many times we missed opportunities to accept the reality of change, to understand its meaning, and to help bring it about in a way that was truly a service to all of mankind. A friend of mine is writing a book now, which will be published here in New York very shortly. He told me that he was going to discuss the Church in relation to seven great revolutions. Think for example, of the Church at the time of the French Revolution; it took a lot of time before we really understood what was the deep positive drive within this movement and to appreciate what was positive in it. The same is true of the Industrial Revolution: Marx's analysis and appreciation of its significance preceded any significant papal document on the same subject by nearly a century. One of our difficulties is that we seem always to be present to life in a negative way. We are well aware of what should not be and we rest content with enunciating that, instead of joining in the effort to formulate what should be. The negative commands of the Decalogue are found, as it were, on the limits of human existence, prescribing the frontiers between humanity and inhumanity and leaving open to the creativity and compassion of man the full wealth of his daily personal decision-making. We have carried this liberating negativity down to the prescription of detailed aspects of human life and, in doing so, we have stifled it.

This negative approach to reality has also created a mentality that easily appreciates the sinfulness of an infraction of a law but cannot understand the morality of sins of omission. Consider Communism — it was not natural that the changes in Russia should have been introduced in opposition to the Church; the Church should have been the leader in that human revolution. Nicholas Berdyaev, an Orthodox Russian Christian, once wrote:

Bolshevism has grown up in Russia, and has been victorious there, because I am what I am [he speaks as a Christian.]; because there was not in me a real spiritual force, the force of a faith capable of moving mountains. Bolshevism is my sin, my fault. It is a trial sent to me. The sufferings that Bolshevism has inflicted on me are for the expiation of my fault, my sin, of our common fault, our common sin. Men, all men are responsible for all men. [7]

This answers in some way, I think, the question that was raised this morning — the problem of corporate sins, most of which are sins of omission. There is as yet very little theological thinking on this problem, but it is certainly an important matter for reflection.

So then, the Church must confront living man where he is and, in the power of the Spirit who is moving toward the Father, bring men to the encounter with the living God. This mandate implies a great openness on the part of the Christian community to all that takes place on this globe. The Church must nevermore appear as an isolated block of humanity preoccupied with its own internal affairs. Of course the Church must be Christ-centered, but Christ Himself, at the center of the Church, is looking out over the whole world and has compassion on the multitude. Love, as Lacordaire once remarked, "is not so much a question of looking at one another, as looking in the same direction." Christ-centeredness, then, implies looking in the same direction as Christ does.

We have to take seriously all the implications of the images our Lord used of the Church, which picture it as immanent in the world. Think, for instance, of the leaven placed by the woman in the dough. It does no good to have leaven next to the dough; it must be *in* it. We mean nothing to anyone if we only hear about human problems; we have to experience them. We have to live as our brothers live if we wish to be credible. The sufferings of our brothers are real and tangible; the problems that bring them anguish are a daily fact of experience. If all we can bring to their suffering are the empty words of some well-rounded formula, we are not only useless — we are laughable.

If the Gospel is the sign-post pointing toward complete human fulfillment, then men have the right to expect from us some deep orientation to the problems we mutually experience. Of course, that is not easy. What are we to say about suffering, death, and morality; or the social problems of racism, war, peace, revolution, development, civil disobedience, urbanism, environment, poverty, pollution? These questions are overwhelming, but we must face them and not try to make religion a desensitizer in the face of the urgency and complexity of these problems. They are there every day for us to see and experience in the people we meet, in the air we breathe, in the newspapers we read, and new dimensions to these problems constantly arise — to mention only one example, think of the actualities and potentialities in the field of genetics. We have to accept these challenges, we have to start where man is to be found. And man is found confronted with these realities. To-day, very often, we begin from the second commandment, love of our neighbor, and in being faithful to it we have our hearts purified and made sensitive to the first commandment — the love of God. Young people today are especially alert to the authenticity of a person's love for his fellow-man and can hardly believe in a God whose worshippers cannot identify in love with their brothers. The rhythm has changed: a few months ago a priest said to me, "When I came out of the seminary, after four years of Theology, I had an answer for every question. But nobody asked me those questions." That's the difference today. We have to start with man's real problems. We have to start with a common ground. We share some values — the value of human dignity and human life, the greatness of freedom of conscience — and we agree in rejecting all those things that militate against the full flowering of humanity. Of course this does not always mean that our dialogue is easy. Sometimes it is difficult to agree on the practical realization of human ideals since there is implied in every such effort a particular view of man, a particular anthropology. It is easier to agree on what is not human, for what is inhuman is not Christian: war is inhuman; there cannot be a Christian war. This doesn't mean that even under this heading we will have an answer ready for every problem, but by the very fact that our minds are clear with regard to our recognition of what is inhuman, we have prepared the

way for dialogue. And in this way the Church is
really in and for the world.

However, the prophetic word that the Church
brings to the world, which can only be communi-
cated when the Church shares humanity with
everyone, is often a word that is against the world,
as Christ opposed the short-sightedness and god-
lessness of the world. Our Lord's image of yeast in
the dough is valid here too: yeast goes against the
tendency of the dough and makes it rise; otherwise the yeast would be overwhelmed by the
dough and would become useless. I think this
truth is especially applicable to us bishops.
Throughout all of history we have had to face the
abiding temptation to be too wise. The hierarchy
is always tempted to mistake appreciation for the
past for a genuine perspective on the future. I am
not saying that we must relinquish all ties with the
past, but simply that we must be on the alert
against our tendency to move in the direction with
which we are more familiar: in the direction of
conservatism.

Today we are tempted to find a sort of compromise with the world; the expression of that
temptation is conformism, just as compromise
with the world of yesterday is immobilism. The
struggle is always with us; we are continually
tempted to let the world overcome the Church. It
is the tension between the leaven and the dough:
if the leaven weakens, it disappears. There is
always this temptation to compromise, the temptation to be too prudent, to find in the world that

confronts us those realities or attitudes that correspond to our own conservative bent, and to label this alliance 'Christian integration.' But prudence is not security, nor is it comfort. Our Lord was a man of unique virtue — He never lacked the virtue of prudence — and he was crucified. Prudence, according to a very fine definition of Father Haring's, is "a calculated choice between two risks." In other words, we have to maintain a very critical stance with regard to the world; we have to judge the world. We bring the light of the Gospel to all these human problems and it may happen that, as we carry this torch of the Gospel, others see better than we do by its light.

Christ is always moving toward the Father, disrupting our many puny human plans, our comfortable religion, which allows us to settle down in our small and selfish notions of what is human. This movement of Christ carries us beyond the world. There is a danger today that Christians will remain within the dimensions of this world. There is a possibility that we, in our belated attempts to be relevant, will accept a closed, secularistic interpretation of life, a 'horizontal' Christianity, a Savior who is little more than an exceptional social worker. We must start from the human and go further, beyond humanity as we experience it, imitating the "philanthropy" of God as the letter of Titus expresses it (Titus 3:4).

We run the risk today of settling for a shortsighted humanitarianism. In the missionary field, for example, there are many young people ready to go to foreign countries to bring technical assistance, but few who want to bring the Gospel. When I say, bring the Gospel, I mean the total message of Christ with all its consequences; a Gospel that could be preached in isolation from the human needs of the people to whom it was addressed would not be Gospel at all. The missionary must express Christ's love and care for human suffering and thus witness to and share His transcendent love for the Father. We have to keep the human and the sacred abreast of one another. We must give people bread and the sacred host; we must teach them the alphabet and the Word of God; we must offer them social security and a deeper sense of God's providence; we must live and teach the value of work and organization and the value of prayer and contemplation. We must save men in their bodies and in their souls; we need social pioneers and saints; that is the call today. We have to bring to mankind that sense that there is more in a man than being man; there is more in humanity than humanity: there is Christ deep within each man and within the human race, Christ who is Himself the leaven of the dough in the mass of humanity, moving man above and beyond what he thinks himself to be. "There is more in you." That is the message we must bring to the world today. As Christ said, "I am coming to give you life, life in abundance." Bringing Christianity means bringing more life, more faith, more hope, more love. Bringing more faith means bringing more light to the world. It means accepting the human light but going further: seeing things that cannot be seen with human eyes. We must go on "seeing the invisible." If you believe, you will see the glory of God, you will see the signs of God, you will see stars where others cannot see them. "The very darkness of faith gives us a clearer perception of the stars in the night, a deeper conviction that day succeeds night and a deeper joy in singing to God who gives songs in the night" (Job 35:10). In the darkness of faith we perceive the real glory of God who is acting in our life, speaking to us in every event and every situation, and establishing with us a permanent dialogue.

We have to bring more light to people through our faith, and we have to bring more hope, saying to people, "There are available to you things you could never dream of." That is the meaning of Christianity, the secret of Christian joy. To confess the faith in this world of today means to have joy. Too many Christians are not joyful. The greatest reproach addressed to any Christian is posed in this question: "Why are you sad? What are you waiting for? If you are really waiting for Christ to come, if every day is bringing you nearer to him, and if you are convinced that he is deep within you, transforming your life into light, then why are you sad?" I recall a famous speech of Newman's in which he spoke of having something to give to humanity, to every man, being able to give hope in every circumstance, even in the face of death. We must not live as though we "had no hope" (I Thessalonians 4:13). We must not only construct a theology of hope, we must be the presence of hope.

The Christian, the Church, must bring to man another kind of love, another quality of love. It is a human love, yes, but we must love not only with our own weak human hearts, but with the heart of Christ within us. We have the duty to love men not only *for* the love of God, but also *with* the love of God. God is working in us, calling us, and all men, with a love that is deeper, more personal, more profound, more practical, and more gentle than men could ever dream of. By living a Christian life we have to bring to the world an abundance of life, of hope and love. At least our union with and our love for all men must be a constant question, forcing men to see and move beyond their own visions and plans. I remember a few days after the death of Pope John, an agnostic was speaking with me and said these words, which I will never forget: "Pope John has made my unbelief uncomfortable." Well, that is what we have to do for the world of today.

6. Ecumenism Today

My intention is to address myself to the question of the Church as a Unity, and that means the question of ecumenism today.

We are living in a time when everything is being discussed and disputed. Everything is a matter for complete re-evaluation, especially by the younger generation. It is very natural, then, that ecumenism should be subject to the same process and that there should be, as it were, a sort of attack against ecumenism. I wish to speak for a while about that rejection of ecumenism and to look at the ecumenical venture from the outside to see what we can do together to respond to the difficulties that are raised. Then I wish to speak at some length about ecumenism in itself, or ecumenism considered from the inside.

Today, wherever there is an international conference or meeting, we can feel the impatience of the young toward the ecumenical movement. This appears every week in some periodical or other. If we consider their objections, I think we can sum them up under four different headings. The new generation objects to ecumenism as we are living it today first of all because youth is always opposed to the past and uninterested in the problems of the past. Ecumenism seems to be just such a problem; an effort characteristic of by-gone days and irrelevant to the present. Second, the younger generation can see no point to ecumenism since it seems to be concerned with resolving doctrinal and theological difficulties and, for a variety of reasons, they are opposed to doctrinal considerations. Third, ecumenical questions are rejected because the Church, in so far as it is an institution, is rejected. The young don't believe that the Holy Spirit works through an institution and they want to leave more freedom for the Holy Spirit and for themselves to move outside the constraining limits of a structure. The fourth objection centers around what is called the "closed Church," that is, the Church preoccupied with internal problems. There is a great insistence that the Church be open to the world and less concerned about its own internal affairs and the relationship of one self-contained group to another.

We have to answer these objections, so let us take them one after the other. There is, first of all, the rejection of the past. This is a typical phenomenon: the young always think that the world began the day they were born, just as the old are sure the world will end when they die. Both are wrong, but men think like that. Not only does

youth reject the past — it simply gives it no
thought; this is especially true of the recent past.
When Eisenhower died, a young man in my
country, about thirty years old, asked me, "Who is
this person, Eisenhower?" The young neither
know the past nor are interested in it. But before
we can reject their stance we have to see what is
true in what they say. An error is always dangerous
because it contains some truth. We must be
sympathetic enough to hear that truth and free it
from what is false.

Those who reject the past are saying quite truly
that reality is in the present; they often see quite
clearly that our vision of this reality is obscured by
the grip that the past holds on us. We must hear
the voice of God speaking today and not insist that
He use the language of yesterday. That is a very
delicate task. On one side we must avoid what
America magazine recently called 'Primitivism,'
the conviction that to find the authentic Church
we must go back to the first century; or that to
understand the split between the East and West,
we must go back to the eleventh century; or that
the Reformation must be viewed only in the
context of the sixteenth century. That would be a
dangerous move and would make of dialogue a
joint archeological expedition. On the other
hand, we must avoid what the same review called
'Presentism,' considering the present moment as
the only reality. The very laws of time would
convict us of error were we to try this. What is
most vital today is outmoded tomorrow. No one
has the slightest desire to read the newspaper of

two days ago, or even yesterday. Things move very quickly. It is the very rapidity of change that points to the necessity of perspective; the new generation, all of whose conscious life has been molded by the speed of modern change, must be helped to see the past as an aid in gaining an overview. It is important, for example, to know that the reform movement of the sixteenth century never intended to create a new Church, but to revivify the one community of believers, the one Church of the past and of always. This kind of perspective and respect for sources is one contribution we can make in our dialogue with the young.

The second objection to ecumenism rests upon the fact that doctrinal problems seem irrelevant. The Lord said, "My words are spirit and life." In my generation we put the accent on the term *spirit* and made of the Lord's words a theological system. Today, youth is more attentive to the other term and emphasizes that the words of Christ are *life*. It insists that Christianity must be practiced, that it must be lived, that orthodoxy must be *orthopraxis.* The young are challenging us and it is good to hear their voice, good to be forced to ask ourselves, "Are we truly integrated Christians? Are our words really our life?" We have been often led to consider doctrine as one part of existence and living as another part, but the doctrine of Christ is like the sun: you cannot separate its light from its warmth. I cannot bring a gospel which is only light: it must be at the same time something that warms the heart and soul and heals human wounds. The young are adamant about this, but at times they insist too strongly. Sometimes their insistence is sheer pragmatism, as if verity were only verification. No, there must be communion in faith. We must follow the injunction of St. Paul and "think alike" (Philippians 2:2). We need theology; we need good theology. When I spoke yesterday about theologians, I was trying to point out the great responsibility of a theologian and the tragedy of his taking his task too lightly. I was stressing the fact that faith is one thing and theology is another. But it is also very important to show today what a great need there is for clear Christian thinking, for truly Spirit-inspired reflection on the life-giving Word. A few years ago at New Delhi, Dr. Ramsey stated this aspect very beautifully when he said, "Good theology is, of itself, ecumenical." Good theology is something that unites, since it is an effort to go beyond the constraining limits of a given culture or intellectual tradition in order to experience the truth. It is important, therefore, to react against the anti-intellectualism of the new generation, but the best answer to their objections is clarity and vitality of thought, not anxious repetition of yesterday's formulas. How important it is that we take seriously those lines we put in the text on ecumenism at the Council, about the hierarchy of truths. This does not mean that one truth is truer than another, but that some truths are central and pertain to the very core of our belief, while others are less directly connected with that core. The young are thinking enough to frame objections against dogmatism; therefore they will listen to someone who is thinking enough to understand their objections in the total context of tradition.

The third difficulty against ecumenism comes from the fact that it appears to the young to be identified with the Church as institution and they reject an institutional Church. They do not believe in all that is of the institution, be it hierarchy, sacramental system, or credal formula. They just say, "We don't need all that, faith is enough; faith is a personal encounter with Christ; an individual experience; not a communitarian dogma." We, all of us, have to show that individualism is not Christianity. We must point out how profoundly Christianity must be a communion of people together with God. We must help the young to see that the social conscience, which they possess to such a marked degree, only reflects that communal dimension of man that is brought to fulfillment in the Body of Christ. To insist upon an individual experience of God and a secular commitment to man is to make of Christianity the enemy of any integral community life. But that contradicts the command of the Lord that we love one another as He loves us, as well as the constant New Testament description of the church as a *Koinonia,* a community. Where you have a community, where you have the people of God together, there must be the service of authority as a point of reference and a guarantee of freedom and mutual cooperation. To insist upon this is simply to draw another, if somewhat practical and humble, conclusion from the insistence today that the Church be *human.*

The final objection against ecumenism concentrates on the contention that it is merely an internal or ecclesiastical affair and that the world has no interest in such intramural preoccupations, but in truly global problems. Here, we might recall all that was said yesterday about the Church as a service to the world. We must always bear in mind that Christ did not come to redeem only the Church, He came to redeem mankind. A few days ago, a theologian expressed this very well when he wrote these lines:

> The Church needs the world to become truly the Church. In ordinary human life we need other people to become ourselves. We can only become ourselves through others. We discover through others who we are and how we respond to love and friendship or hatred and hostility. If we need others and are involved with others in love and in work, we come to self-knowledge and some kind of possession of ourselves, and then truly become ourselves. It seems to me that the Christian Church also is in need of others to become herself. God is indeed the God of the Church, but he is also the God of history and the God of the world, and He is at work in us and among us, not only through word and sacrament, but also through our dialogue with other churches and with the world. I think that it is a great challenge to us, a challenge to the way we educate our young people and a challenge to the way we plan the ecumenical movement in the future. [8]

So, let us go on now to consider this ecumenical movement.

Wonderful things have been happening in the

Church of God in these recent years. Something wonderful happened when the World Council of Churches started and something wonderful happened when Pope John appeared and created a whole new dialogue. I think we can apply to him, as I did in the homily I gave in St. Peter's after his death, the text, "There was a man sent from God whose name was John." When he received the observers at Vatican II the first week, he spoke very simple and plain words: "We do not intend," he said, "to conduct a trial of the past; we do not want to prove who was right or who was wrong; the blame was on both sides. All we want to say is, 'Let us come together, let us make an end to our divisions.' " And you remember how Pope John used to say, "Some people always want to complicate simple matters; I wish to simplify complicated matters." At the beginning of the Council, and very frequently thereafter, he used to say, "I don't know where we are going. Let us just follow day by day what the Holy Spirit will ask us to do. In this business of Councils, we are all novices and the Holy Spirit knows it."

So then, as we view ecumenism from within, I should say that some very important things have now begun in the area of what I would like to call doctrinal convergence. His Grace spoke this morning about some specific problems in which there is an ever growing consensus. There is a real consensus coming about between the theologians, especially between Anglican and Catholic theologians in regard to the Eucharist, Scripture and Tradition, in regard to collegiality, and in the relationship between the Word of God and Sacraments. Just before coming here I had the joy of reading the text which expresses some of the agreements in the theological field reached by both parties. One can feel that the Holy Spirit is at work. If we are uncomfortable in the Church today, it is because the Holy Spirit is moving us out of our familiar, irreconcilable positions into a deeper and closer union. When you think about it, it is a wonder that we can speak together at all when we consider the centuries that have elapsed before our dialogue began. I remember asking a good friend of mine, the Orthodox theologian Andrew Scrima, who was the delegate of Patriarch Athenagoras at Vatican II, "What do you think is the main obstacle to the reunion of the Orthodox Church and the Catholic Church?" He answered, "It seems to me that the main obstacle is that we did not speak to one another for nine centuries." There are other experiences that serve to illustrate the same tragedy. During the war, in my country, families were separated for four years, some living on this side of the world and some on the other; they were exposed to different influences, heard a different version of the news, shared different reactions. At the end of the war it often took a long time to reestablish a true unity within the same family. We have to learn again that dialogue means listening. I think that the more we say to one another, "Tell us how it seems to you," the more we will say, "But that is exactly what I see, too, but often because my stress is different, I forget to say it."

Of course, there are still areas of obscurity and stumbling blocks. We have to face these, hoping that in these areas, too, some progress will be made. I have in mind especially two difficult problems, Papal Primacy and Collegiality; and also the problem of Catholic Mariology. In these areas there is something yet to be clarified. In regard to the primacy and infallibility of the Pope, I would like to quote here a few lines from a letter from Newman to Miss Holmes after Vatican I. In the wake of Vatican I the impression was created that the Pope had absorbed all the Church and outside of Papal authority there was no true authority in the Church. Right after Vatican I, Newman wrote these words:

" . . . we must have a little faith. Abstract propositions avail little . . . . No truth stands by itself — each is kept in order and harmonized by other truths. The dogmas relative to the Holy Trinity and the Incarnation were not struck off all at once — but piecemeal — one Council did one thing, another a second — and so the whole dogma was built up. And the first portion of it looked extreme — and controversies rose upon it — and these controversies led to the second, and third Councils, and they did not *reverse* the first, but *explained* and *completed* what was first done. So it will be now. Future Popes will explain and in one sense limit their own power." [9]

As we have seen, Newman's words were partially fulfilled at Vatican II. I am thinking of some particularly important aspects of this question: for instance, when we stressed the sacramentality of the episcopate. It was very important to show that the episcopate does not derive from papal delegation, but that it comes directly from Christ. The Council also invited us to stress, once again, that Christ alone is the head of the Church and that we should reserve this term for Christ, using some other phrase to express the role of the Pope, such as, "visible center of unity." I think there was a step in the right direction also in the development of the theology of local Churches. In the years to come, we will clarify and develop this direction of thinking so that the Church will appear as a communion of local Churches and we will return to a greater fidelity to a Pauline understanding of this notion. Though Paul spoke about the Church of Corinth or Ephesus or elsewhere, he still used the singular, Church, when speaking of the total reality in this world. That is, the mystery of the Church, the Church of God, is a unity in its very origin and at the same time it is a plurality. It is a union of communities bound together and sharing in the one reality which they together make up. We must not be afraid of plurality because plurality and unity are both essential dimensions of the Church.

The notion of collegiality met with some difficulties at the Council but even there progress was evident. But perhaps the most important revolution at the Council, the one with the greatest ecumenical consequences, was the reversal of the order of Chapters II and III of the Constitution on the Church. Originally the first three chapters were in this order: Chapter I: The Church as a Mystery; Chapter II: The Church as a Hierarchy;

Chapter III: The Church as the People of God. Then someone proposed to me (I was the relator) that the order of the chapters be inverted. I accepted the suggestion. I saw something in what he was saying, but just something. Now, everyday I discover more profoundly that it was the genius of the Holy Spirit that changed the order of these chapters and thus brought to the forefront the reality that the Church is the people of God together: all the baptized living together in coresponsibility. Then there is the hierarchy made up of some of these people of God dedicated to a particular service of the rest. I think the more that we realize this and live it out, the more ecumenism will evolve in the Church today.

Yes, we are making progress, but it is not without a struggle. Within each one of us, and within the Church as a whole, there is still a battle to be waged against inertia, ignorance, and prejudice. We are still on pilgrimage, and at times the weather is a bit stormy, just as it can be here in New York. From time to time, you have to make a special effort and insist upon one aspect or another of a truth. If we consider some events that followed upon the Council in this line of ecumenism, we have, first of all, the first synod of bishops. Two hundred of us met in Rome. We came together to discuss some problems, but the most important fruit of that meeting was the creation of an international commission of theologians: a balanced selection of the best catholic theologians in the world. I think that is a very important step for the future of ecumenism. At the second synod in 1969, we asked that this commission study the problems of Papacy, Primacy, and Collegiality. The second synod was certainly a step forward in the practice of collegiality. This was especially marked by a creation of a permanent synodal commission of fifteen bishops surrounding the Pope. I was asked by journalists, "Are you pleased with Synod II?" I answered by using a comparison: "Well, it is like an elevator. If you see an elevator at the second floor of a building, which has twenty floors, you can say, 'It is only at the second floor,' or you can say, 'It is already at the second floor.'" So, I think we have left the ground and collegiality is a real thing now. But you must not be disturbed if progress is not easy; we are on the road, we are moving. It is not so much a question of discussing theological distinctions; it is certainly not a question of legalism. You cannot express the rights of the Pope and the rights of the bishops in neat legal categories. It is a question of communion in faith and in action and that is not easy to define, though the experience of its presence is unmistakable. We are definitely moving in the direction of communion and therefore losing an easy capacity to express ourselves in more familiar legal and theological terminology. The more we move in this direction, the more closely we touch upon the mystery of the Church. Dr. Ramsey expressed this very well when he wrote:

> For a primacy should depend upon and express the organic authority of the Body; and the discovery of its precise functions will come not by discussion of the Petrine claims in isolation but by the recovery

everywhere of the Body's organic life, with its
Bishops, presbyters and people. In this Body Peter
will find his due place, an ultimate reunion is
hastened not by the pursuit of 'the Papal controversy' but by the quiet growth of the organic life
of every part of Christendom. [10]

I think that if, on every level of the Church, we
seriously accept coresponsibility, the Pope with
the bishops, the bishops with the Pope, and if the
bishops, individually, are earnestly coresponsible
with their priests, their deacons, and the laity, and
if each individual bishop understands and accepts
his role as the focal point of unity for the local
Church, then the solution to our problems will
emerge. The more each bishop and each member
of the Church opens himself in faith to the reality
of coresponsibility, the more will we be able to
solve problems that at this moment seem insur-
mountable. We have to do what Zeno once did
when grappling with the problem of motion:
"Solvitur eundo."

And finally, I wish you courage and faith on this
road of ecumenism. It was such a joy for me to be
with you and to think aloud with you as we move
in the same direction, desiring the same goals and
praying for that visible unity that is the will of the
Lord. May we know the experience of the disciples on their way to Emmaus who, as they
walked along side by side, were "talking together"
— literally, "seeking together" — when the Lord
appeared to them.

There is no doubt that the Spirit of the Lord is
urging us on. Each generation must take up the

pilgrim's staff and continue the search for God's truth about His Church. We are committed to exploring continually the riches of revelation. It will be a rare joy to be able at the end of our pilgrimage to repeat these words of the poet:

We shall not cease from exploration
And the end of all our exploring
Will be to arrive where we started
And know the place for the first time. [11]

NOTES

[1] Yves Congar, *Dialogue Between Christians* (London: Geoffrey Chapman Limited, 1966; Paramus, N.J.: Paulist/Newman Press, 1967), pp. 95-97.

[2] Antoine de St. Exupery, *Wind, Sand and Stars,* translated by Lewis Galantiere (New York: Harcourt, Brace and World, 1949), p. 60.

[3] Arthur A. Vogel, *Is the Last Supper Finished: Sacred Light on a Sacred Meal* (New York: Sheed and Ward, 1968), p. 120.

[4] (New York: Harcourt, Brace and World, 1933), p. 229.

[5] Archpriest Armand J. Jacopin, "In the Eastern Christian View Christmas Is the Festival of Re-creation," *The Catholic Messenger* (Davenport, Iowa), December 18, 1969.

[6] Quoted by Bernard Basset in *We Agnostics: On the Tightrope to Eternity* (New York: Herder and Herder, 1968), p. 89.

[7] Nicholas Berdyaev, *Un Nouveau Moyen-Age* (Paris, 1930), pp. 186-187.

[8] Gregory Baum, "Ecumenism and the Catholic Church," *World Outlook,* June 1967, p. 22. This idea is further developed in Baum's *Man Becoming* (New York: Herder and Herder, 1970), pp. 51-54.

[9] Letter of May 15, 1871, to Miss Mary Holmes, quoted in Wilfrid Ward, *The Life of John Henry Cardinal Newman* (London: Longmans, Green and Co., 1912), II, 379.

[10] *The Gospel and the Catholic Church* (2nd Ed.; London: Longmans, Green and Co., 1956), p. 229.

[11] T. S. Eliot, "Little Gidding," *Four Quartets* (London: Faber and Faber Ltd.; New York: Harcourt, Brace and World, 1943).